Money Management

The Ultimate Guide to Budgeting, Frugal Living, Getting out of Debt, Credit Repair, and Managing Your Personal Finances in a Stress-Free

© Copyright 2019

All Rights Reserved. No part of this book may be reproduced in any form without permission in writing from the author. Reviewers may quote brief passages in reviews.

Disclaimer: No part of this publication may be reproduced or transmitted in any form or by any means, mechanical or electronic, including photocopying or recording, or by any information storage and retrieval system, or transmitted by email without permission in writing from the publisher.

While all attempts have been made to verify the information provided in this publication, neither the author nor the publisher assumes any responsibility for errors, omissions or contrary interpretations of the subject matter herein.

This book is for entertainment purposes only. The views expressed are those of the author alone, and should not be taken as expert instruction or commands. The reader is responsible for his or her own actions.

Adherence to all applicable laws and regulations, including international, federal, state and local laws governing professional licensing, business practices, advertising and all other aspects of doing business in the US, Canada, UK or any other jurisdiction is the sole responsibility of the purchaser or reader.

Neither the author nor the publisher assumes any responsibility or liability whatsoever on the behalf of the purchaser or reader of these materials. Any perceived slight of any individual or organization is purely unintentional.

Contents

PART 1: MONEY MANAGEMENT 0
INTRODUCTION 1
CHAPTER 1: THE MONEY MINDSET 3
CHAPTER 2: DEBT - GETTING OUT OF IT AND HOW 12
CHAPTER 3: BUDGETING FOR BEGINNERS 42
CHAPTER 4: SIMPLE WAYS TO SAVE EVERY DAY 72
CHAPTER 5: INVESTING FOR BEGINNERS 91
CONCLUSION 104
PART 2: CREDIT REPAIR 105
INTRODUCTION 106
CHAPTER 1: BOOSTING YOUR CREDIT SCORE 108
CHAPTER 2: PAYING OFF DEBT 149
CHAPTER 3: SAVING MONEY 179
CHAPTER 4: MANAGING YOUR PERSONAL FINANCES IN A STRESS-FREE WAY 194
CONCLUSION 210

Part 1: Money Management

An Essential Guide on How to Get out of Debt and Start Building Financial Wealth, Including Budgeting and Investing Tips, Ways to Save and Frugal Living Ideas

Introduction

Have you ever wondered how some people earn a small income, and they never complain about it, and then some have a lot of money, but they can't manage to pay their monthly bills? Or how millionaires manage their money?

One of the most important steps towards being independent is financial independence. This means you are in total control of your expenses and the money you make.

Money is crucial when it comes to living well in the community, but you don't need too much money to become independent, happy, or even successful. You merely need to know how to control your expenses and manage the money you have so that it can work for you.

Debts can be a source of worry and anxiety for many people, and sometimes, it can be tough to know where to start when you want to manage your financial debts. This book will help you to get started on the path to paying off all your debts and become debt free. The book will provide you with a clear picture of how much money you owe, and to whom, how you can contact credit card companies and negotiate interest rates, how you can prioritize which debt to pay off first, which strategy to adopt to clear your debts, and how to create a budget. Also, the book is meant to teach you the most important aspects of personal finance.

Besides that, you will further learn how to get started with investments and make sure that your money works for you, and not the other way around. You will be taken through many exciting tips and lessons that you should follow to fulfill your financial goals. Get ready to learn interesting stuff, including how you can become debt free without much hassle.

Chapter 1: The Money Mindset

Do you have a massive debt? Are you feeling stressed about paying your debts? Do you struggle to make ends meet? Do you find it hard to pay your monthly bills? Do you find it hard to save? Are you living in fear of losing your home?

If you answered "yes" to any of the above questions, you aren't alone. According to the United States Census Bureau, it is estimated that more than 69% of Americans are in debt. Also, colleges students are said to have, on average, $35,000 in student loans.

Everyone has gone through a financial crisis at one point in their life, including the wealthiest people in the world. Debt can be overwhelming, and if not handled well, it can lead to depression. If you are one of those people who is experiencing a financial crisis, keep in mind that no problem is permanent. In fact, there are numerous options that you can take to start fixing this problem.

Many people want to be debt free, but borrowing money is not a bad thing. Debt can be good or bad; it just depends on how you look at it.

Despite this, debt has been linked to negative connotations. Most people cast down their heads when the talk of debt emerges; some even feel embarrassed about it. If you let debt control your life, then it can generate more and more anxiety.

Debt happens; it is part of life. It is not a bad thing like the way people perceive it. In particular, debt causes a positive effect. Just because someone owes you money, doesn't mean that you are financially struggling. What is important is how you approach it.

When feeling low about your financial problems, just remember that debt can be a means of buying a home that you have always dreamed of. In other words, not all debts are equal. If you are already in debt or you're worried about getting into debt, read on to learn more. Understanding debt is vital to both financial security and financial literacy.

Debt is not a life sentence. It can be a way for you to examine your financial priorities and adjust your life.

Debt is debt until you give it meaning

One of the life-changing magic points from Brooke Castillo originates from a famous quote: "Your thoughts create your feelings. Your feelings create your actions. Your actions create your results. Circumstances are neutral."

So in simple terms, Brooke Castillo is saying,

Thoughts=>Feelings=>Actions=>Results.

Brooke's quote simply sums up how the universe operates. If you go to learn about personal development and psychology, you'll learn the same thing. In other words, it is not made-up stuff by Brooke, but he nicely polished it.

Indeed, circumstances are neutral. They are neither good nor bad. They are simply facts.

If you still have problems in understanding this, read these two examples.

First, consider a peach. You might love peaches, and someone else hates them. Neither is the peach good nor bad; it is just a peach. The peach doesn't turn bad or good until we consider it bad.

Secondly, let's look at the idea of death. Many people die every day. However, we are unaffected by it. And we have to be. There is no option. We can't go around being depressed about losing people we don't know. But the fact remains that people are dying. We grieve when someone we love passes on. Why? Because we have taken the time to think about death. We have given death meaning. This applies to everything.

Going back to where we left off, circumstances are neutral. You have the power to make them mean whatever you think about. And debt is not an exception. In other words, debt is neutral. Neither bad nor good.

In particular, your current debt is neutral. This doesn't mean going into debt in the coming years, which would be an action. We are talking about the debt you're already in.

This is good news.

Why? Because you can choose what you want your debt to mean.

It doesn't matter what your lover, best friend, mom, or cousin say about your debt—it's up to you to make it mean whatever you want.

When you choose debt to mean something bad about you, it's you who is going to suffer

Many people have made debt mean so much about them in an unproductive way. Little do they know that they are hurting themselves. Many people feel embarrassed to talk about their debts. Some consider themselves hopeless because of debt. Then there is the scarcity mindset.

This is where you start to think that there is not enough money, not enough love, and not enough time. And when you start to think this way, that is the type of reality that you create. Then your brain starts to prove what you are thinking.

So, if you think that your debt is the obstacle to achieving what you want to attain in life and that you can't have the successful financial future you always dreamed of, then it will be so.

"Yes," you'll be saying, "I want to do all the things I have outlined in life, but I don't have money in the bank because of my debt."

Rather than waste time thinking about what you cannot achieve or have because of your debt, think about what is possible with your debt.

This is defined as abundant thinking. If you don't know, it is the way you believe that there is always enough time, enough money, and enough of everything.

Right, you have a debt. So what?

By feeling like it has happened to you, it will not assist you at all. However, if you ask what your debt can do, it will help you.

The way you feel about debt defines your actions

Whatever you decide to believe about your debt will determine how you are going to think about debt.

Keep in mind that your thoughts create feelings. Your feelings will trigger your actions. Finally, your efforts will trigger your results.

For instance, if you feel that your debt is shameful, then you may experience embarrassment.

If you believe that debt is someone else's fault, then you will experience self-pity and identify as a victim.

However, if you think that your debt is an opportunity, then you will feel empowered. Whatever it is that you think about your debt will define the way you think of it.

The way you feel about debt is more important than anything else because it generates action.

Be attentive to the way you feel about your debt; it is more important than anything.

To choose the way you feel about your debt, decide how you want the result to become and work backward.

For instance, if the result is to become debt free from the point of abundance, then you want to think your debt is an opportunity. This will cause you to feel empowered, which will cause you to take action and get out of debt.

If you are yet to understand how this works, then you will need to put it into action and get your results. You will lose nothing by trying it. Your brain enjoys solving problems. If you ask yourself, "How can I turn this debt into an opportunity?" each night before you go to sleep, you will see an improvement and new means of thinking. Your brain will start working to find answers.

Similarly, you could feel embarrassed about your debt. Concentrate on reducing all your expenses and scaling to the point where you will be living in total deprivation and feeling like crap. Still, you can get out of debt this way, but it would be from the point of scarcity.

This doesn't mean that going frugal is a bad thing or that it's not the way you need to do it. The tactic isn't that important. The most important thing is the beliefs and feelings behind the actions.

Keep in mind that it is better to think and feel in a particular manner that provides you with the changes you want from a place of abundance.

Developing the correct mindset about debt

If you want to live debt free, you will need to do something more apart from practicing good money management practices. It is also about building the right mindset to help you get out of debt.

Debt requires diligence and dedication. However, mental strength is one overlooked technique that can be applied to trigger motivation and attain success faster.

Amy Morin, a psychotherapist and author, says, "Your thoughts affect the way you feel and the way you act." She goes on to add, "If you think paying off debt looks overwhelming and painful, you won't succeed." However, with some quick mind tricks, you can deal with worries and reduce debt.

And the first step is to change your mindset if you want to free yourself from the burden of debt.

Below are four significant insights that you should develop regarding the mindset to get out of debt:

1. Not just about money

Many people think that the major problem of being in debt is the amount of money that they need to pay to creditors and banks. They imagine all the interest that they will have to pay. Or they bemoan the large payments and other types of charges connected to the debt.

But the right "price tag" for debt is far from the financial expense; it is the level of pain that debt brings to your life.

The debt will affect your emotional status, leading to depression. Debt affects relationships, causing couples to fight, argue, or even worse, divorce. Debts restrict your personal growth and career options, making it difficult for you to move because of the vast money you need to pay for your mortgage or credit cards.

2. Acknowledge your debt

Many people who have debts either don't acknowledge it or are unsure about the total amount.

This is the time to face the facts and become open on how much and the type of debt you have. As it is always said, you can't fix a problem until you accept it. Don't wait for your creditors to begin the intervention process—develop your own. This will also assist you in creating a personal responsibility mindset. And it is the best for not just paying your debts but also staying out of debt.

Take a piece of paper or even look for a spreadsheet and write down all your debts, such as a car loan, credit card, and student loans. You can't afford to fail to know these details.

3. Accept the debt, forgive yourself and move on

You will not be a human if your emotions won't rise when you look at the total of your debts. There will, at least, be some level of guilt, anger, regret, and maybe some embarrassment. Take the time to feel whatever it is that you are feeling. The right mindset to help you approach your debts and clear them is an honest one where you take responsibility. If you are trapped in a blame mindset, you will find it very difficult to break the debt cycle.

Don't attempt to sweep any emotions under the rug; accept them so that you can move on to the next stage. This is also the best time to think about why you accumulated the debt. Was it because of uncontrolled spending? Maybe you were out of work, and you had to live off your credit card/s. Whatever reason, resolve it to avoid it from taking place.

Some of us learn best by making mistakes. So consider this debt a lesson learned and move forward.

4. It is no one's fault

Humans like to blame others for their debts and financial problems, i.e., the "irresponsible" wife or husband who mismanaged the bills or the "stingy" boss who wouldn't increase the salary or even the "greedy" bankers who send out loans and credit.

To eliminate debt, you need to understand your responsibility and become motivated. You need to start to consider the decisions you have made and actions that caused the current status.

It is just by seeing your responsibility that you become empowered. You need to begin to think, *I got myself into this mess so I can get myself out of it.* When you are at your best, you need to ask yourself, "How did I contribute to my debt?" And most importantly, "What can I do to turn things around?"

Still, if you already have debt, keep in mind that this is not your fault; you could have gone through various life challenges like a divorce, so you need to assess whatever happened, and start to plan how you can secure your home against unexpected events.

Would it have been possible to have significant savings? Would you have had enough insurance? Rather than blame others, concentrate on what you can currently do to prevent any other problem from happening.

5. Let go of limiting beliefs

These are beliefs that prevent certain behaviors and actions and restrict people from fulfilling their goals. For those that don't believe in their potential to overcome debt, Payne-Stanley recommends writing down any thoughts that act as a barrier to clear them.

Payne-Stanely says that when you let go of limiting beliefs, you feel relieved and not weighed down by thoughts and ideas that keep you trapped in debt.

6. **Debt is temporary**

The debt that you currently have can be a temporary setback and cleared by establishing the best mindset to deal with debt, and that involves taking personal responsibility. Just ensure that you continue to maintain that mindset so that you don't fall back into the old actions that generated the debt.

If you are addicted to shopping, find a solution to it, or you will be back in debt again before you realize it. If your income is erratic, look for means to create other ways of earning income, such as a side hustle.

Create a budget and stick to it, and assign yourself splurge cash so that you can maintain a positive mindset and continue saving.

Remember to celebrate your wins no matter how small they may be because they are worth celebrating. Your long-term success relies on changing your mindset from the one that got you into debt in the first place.

Chapter 2: Debt - Getting Out of It and How

Are you tired of paying your credit card bills? Do you want to learn how you can clear all your debts?

If you want a long-lasting solution to your debt, then you need to know that the financial problem does not cause your debt. Debt is a personal issue. However, most people look for financial solutions as a means to pay their debt. For that reason, they never get to address the primary cause of their debt.

The Permanent Debt Solution

A clear definition and interpretation of your debt are vital to finding a solution for it. That is where most debtors start by going wrong. They define debt as a financial problem, and hence, begin to look for financial solutions.

That explains why their debt woes keep coming back even after paying the debt off. In other words, they don't address the root cause of the debt, and this creates a channel for the problem to repeat.

But a long-lasting solution needs a solid plan that takes advantage of a working principle. When you partially reduce your debt balance, you only limit the pain symptoms. However, the main issue still exists. In other words, you are already in debt.

The leading cause of debt is personal life attitudes and habits that result in too much spending. So, the right thing to do is to address your life instead of the financial sides of life.

That's an important principle. By understanding this principle, you can then solve your debt woes permanently.

Dealing With the Symptom Rather Than the Cause

When you feel some pain or have a stomachache, the first thing that you will always want to do is to look for some medicine to relieve the pain. Unfortunately, this doesn't treat the real cause of the stomachache, and so the underlying problems remain.

It is the same thing with debt. Many people know that they need to earn more and spend less so that they can pay their debt. As a result, they try to concentrate their energy on financially-driven solutions.

A permanent solution is to change the attitudes and way of living that led to the problem. But remember, you are the cause of the debt, and so it is up to you to come up with the solution.

The financial issues you experience reflect the wrong financial decisions you make. Sometimes, you aren't even aware of these decisions.

For that reason, teaching a debtor to cut down on his or her expenditure is equivalent to urging someone to reduce weight by doing a lot of exercise and reducing their food intake.

Most people know the answer to getting out of debt; the only challenge is that they don't know how to implement the actions.

The Habits That Can Cause Your Debt

Most debt problems are emotional. This is the reason why you will see people who buy things that they can't afford or even spend more than what they earn.

The basic principle in finance requires a person to limit their spending. They should spend less than the amount of money they earn. However, this is not easy to implement as it sounds. Well, how can a person avoid emotional barriers that lead to more debt?

The simplest means is to start by adopting good financial habits that will reduce the distance between what you need to do and how you can implement it. This way, you can be sure to make a step in reducing your debt. By adopting new habits, you will be able to make quality decisions that will lead to a pleasant financial outcome.

The best thing is that you are the one to determine your financial condition regardless of your position today. You create habits, and the habits lead to long-term financial success. In other words, you will be in charge of everything, including the ability to make positive improvements.

Below are six habits that you should consider. These habits will determine your financial success.

1. Emotional spending

Here is a simple test that will help you know whether you are an "emotional spender":

- Do you celebrate by shopping for a treat?
- Do you shop for social connection?
- Do you have more than one of the same product/s?
- Do you shop for entertainment?
- Do you go shopping to manage stress?
- Do you feel anxious, guilty, or remorseful when shopping?
- Do you hide your purchases from loved ones or friends?
- Do you shop for purposes of "retail therapy"?

If you said "yes" to any of the above questions, then you are experiencing an emotional spending issue.

As an emotional shopper, you like to buy things that will make you feel good. This is a big problem because it can make you develop a physiological habit.

As a result, you may find yourself excessively buying things that you necessarily don't need to buy. The right thing to do here is to learn to buy things based on your needs. Make sure that you plan for something to buy instead of spontaneous shopping.

If you want to break the cycle of emotional shopping, give yourself a two-day break without going to shop whenever you want something. If you still need to buy the same item after two days, then it could be worth it to go and buy it.

2. Addiction

It is quite similar to emotional spending. Addiction could be of any type, not necessarily shopping. Because of the addiction, you will need to buy whatever you are addicted to. The result is that you increase your debt.

The wealthy habit is to stay away from any form of addiction and live healthily. If you experience addiction problems, you will need to look for some professional assistance.

3. Entitlement

This happens when you start to believe that you need all the great things in life no matter your financial capability. Entitlement causes you to look for the latest phones, TVs, cars, and designer clothes. The right step to make to avoid entitlement is to buy only things that you can pay depending on the strength of your pocket.

4. Immediate gratification

If you are one of those people who always want something now, and you are even ready to pay for it instantly, then you are suffering from instant gratification.

It is important to train yourself to seek for delayed gratification. One way is to learn to pay cash for anything that you want to buy instead of using a credit card.

5. Self-worth associated with stuff

Advertisements often try to persuade you to believe that a particular product will add value to your life. You could either feel happier or look smarter in a given product. It is easy to get convinced by this kind of belief—little do you know that you will be plunging yourself into massive debt.

The right thing that you should do is to learn to separate your feelings from self-worth. Keep in mind that possessions don't define your worth. Ask yourself why you spend. Are you trying to satisfy a contrived want or genuine need? Keep this advice: the things you want don't define your worth as a human being.

6. Complacency

Nothing increases the occurrence of debt more than complacency. The attitude of the debtor could be, "I'm already in debt, so what's the big deal if I spend a little more?"

Complacency is one of the most dangerous things because the good feelings when you buy a product are different from the pain your experience when you want to pay the credit card bills.

You need to teach yourself to respond proactively for any cautionary signs of an incoming financial problem.

Common Types of Debt and How to Tackle Them

Accumulating debt might seem like falling into a deep hole and trying to find your way out without anything to hold on to. However, there are some methods that you can depend upon to help you pay off your debt. This section teaches you how to get started.

Before starting to look at how you can tackle common types of debts, it is vital that you familiarize yourself with some of the terms that are used to define debt. This will help you to know what you have:

- **Secured debt**

These are the types of debts that are protected using an asset such as a car or house. In this case, the asset acts as collateral. A lien is assigned on the asset by lenders, permitting them to repossess the asset if the borrower is unable to pay the debt. When the lender seizes the asset, it is usually sold at an auction. When the price sold doesn't cover the whole debt, the lender can pursue the borrower for the remaining balance known as a deficiency balance.

Auto loan and mortgage loan are a few categories of secured loans. Your property or home protects your mortgage loan. If you fail to pay these loans, the lender can seize the property. A title loan is another form of secured debt because the debt has been secured with a title to another asset.

You cannot fully own an asset linked to a secured debt until the time when you have finished paying the loan. At that moment, you can request the lender to release the asset and grant you the title that is free of any liens.

- **Unsecured Debts**

For unsecured debts, there is no permission granted to any collateral for the debt. This means that if you fail to pay the debt, they cannot come to repossess your assets.

Though they can't seize your property as a repayment plan, alternative actions can be taken to force you to pay the debt. For instance, they can employ a debt collector to persuade you to complete the debt. If this fails to work, the lender can decide to sue you and request the court to "garnish your wages", seize your asset, or place a lien on your assets until the time when you clear your debt. They can also report you to the credit bureaus so that the delinquent payment reflects on the credit report. Similarly, lenders of secured debts can also take the above actions.

The most common example of unsecured debt is the credit card debt loan. Other examples of unsecured debt include payday loans, medical bills, and student loans.

- **Fixed interest rate debt**

This is a debt instrument such as a gilt-edged bond or debenture that investors use to lend money to a company to get interested. Fixed interest security has a specified interest rate that cannot change in the course of the instrument. The face value is paid when the security matures.

The trust indenture has the fixed-interest security that is paid on fixed-interest security. This is paid until the bond matures. The advantage of fixed interest security is that investors are already aware of how much interest they are going to earn for the duration of the bond's life. Provided the issuing party doesn't default for the period of the bond's life, the investor can calculate the estimate of his or her return.

However, this kind of debt is also prone to interest risk. Given that their interest rate is constant, these securities shall depreciate as the prices increase in a rising-interest-rate condition. In case the cost of interest drops, the fixed-interest security increases in value.

For these types of debts, they are not riskier than equities. Despite this, bondholders are said to be unsecured creditors. Thus, they may not receive all their principal back.

Variable interest rate debt

In a nutshell, this particular interest rate is related to a key interest rate called index. Any changes to the index will affect the interest rate that you pay for loans, and that will also change. Having a variable interest rate can result in excessive spending to clear your debt than you had planned. Before you choose a new variable rate loan, it is important to read the terms.

When you select a new credit card or a new loan, you can take it for granted that the rate of interest will always remain the same. But that's not necessarily true.

Certain financial products have a variable interest rate; this means that the amount of interest you have to pay on the money that you borrow can be subjected to some periodic changes.

Most financial products have a variable interest rate; this includes:

1. Auto loans
2. Student private loans
3. Credit cards

Lenders can cut the variable rates as a response to essential indexes, such as the prime rate. When the index which your variable interest rate is connected to changes, your lender can decide to change the interest rate. And when this happens, your monthly payment can rise or drop.

However, not all loans have variable rates. In case a loan has a fixed interest rate, this means that it will not be subject to the same changes in an index rate.

If you select a loan that has a variable interest rate, it can be a financial risk, but on some rare occasions, it can be a better choice than the fixed-rate mortgage.

How often does the rate change?

The changes in the rate of interest depend on the terms of financing and the index rate that your lender is based on. For instance, credit cards are commonly linked to the "The Wall Street Journal's U.S. prime rate", which is the benchmark rate for corporate loans. The number of interest rate changes that you get subjected to can change significantly. For instance:

- Variable-rate credit cards usually change simultaneously with the Federal Reserve changes to the federal funds rate, which can take place several times in a year.
- The variable-rate of student loans can change every time.
- Adjustable-rate mortgages usually remain the same for the first three-five years, and later change periodically.

Can I be notified when my rate is changing?

The "Truth in Lending Act" ensures that you know all information related to interest rates before you close a loan. As a result, it is the responsibility of the lender to reveal the APR whether it is variable or fixed when you register for an auto or mortgage loan.

For certain loans, you will also get a notice before each rate changes. In the adjustable-rate mortgage, your loan servicer is supposed to deliver to you a notice at least seven months before the rise in your mortgage payment. Next, you'll be notified two-four months early of every payment when the change affects your monthly fee.

The "Truth in Lending Act" requires all creditors to have information about your APR and determine whether it is fixed or variable before you register for a credit card.

Issuers of credit card aren't supposed to notify you when your variable rate is about to change, but some do it voluntarily.

At what time is the variable rate best?

The variable interest rates can be quite risky. When your debt payment rises every month, or even annually, it can make things hard to stick to a budget. But sometimes, a variable rate may be the best for you.

Variable-rate credit cards

Most credit card APRs aren't fixed, so you might have no choice apart from going for a variable-rate card. Unlike loans, you can avoid any interest on goods you purchase using credit cards by clearing your balance before the due date every month or during a 0% interest introductory time.

When the index linked to your rate rises, the credit issuer can decide to apply for the increase to pre-existing balances. Most credit card companies charge the increased interest for the whole billing cycle, even when the index only increased towards the end of the cycle.

The variable-rate loans

The rate on variable-rate loans may reduce when the indexes drop, but adjustable-rate mortgages don't always follow the same pattern. Some may even place limits on the amount your interest can fall.

But under the correct conditions, a variable-rate loan can be more cost-effective than a fixed-rate loan.

The reason is that the interest rate on variable loans can begin much lower compared to fixed-rate loans, and then it can rise over time. For the adjustable-rate mortgages that have an initial fixed-rate period, if you know that you are going to flip a home or even sell it before the rates significantly increase, a variable rate can save you money.

However, if you stay in the house beyond the fixed-rate period, your payments can drastically increase. This could make it difficult to pay down your balance.

All in all, a variable interest rate can increase the entire debt repayment. That's the reason why you need to pay attention to the interest rates and run some comparisons before you apply.

Before you choose a new variable-rate method, whether it's a mortgage or credit card, just ensure that you are ready for the interest rate and monthly payments. When you are prepared for this, it can assist you in knowing whether your budget can remain stable during a worst-case scenario.

Fixed payment terms

This is where the terms of the payment define the due date for the payment. The benchmark date is determined and extracted from the payment terms that are used as the benchmark to determine the due date for the payment.

Variable repayment period

Variable repayment interest is set to change now and then. This means that it will rise and fall throughout the mortgage. In other words, the repayment might change in the entire mortgage term. You can set extra repayments to the variable rate mortgage at any period.

Deductible

This type of loan is suitable for a personal circumstance, and hence, may contain tax benefits such as a mortgage or even student loan.

Non-deductible

A type of loan that is usually used to buy a rising asset or a new skill such as personal loans or credit cards.

Credit cards

Regardless of how painful it can be, you need to have a record of all your credit card debt. Write down your debt plus the interest rate for every card. Get in touch with every issuer and offer them a detailed description of the reason you are unable to pay and the amount you can manage.

You also need to try to discuss with them how they can reduce the interest on each of your credit cards. A one-point reduction will still allow you to cut down on the debt.

After you know the size of the debt that you have to pay back, determine the length of time you will take. This will assist you in setting a period and a breakdown of how you are going to pay at the end of each month.

In case you have a tight budget, you can start by paying the least expense each month, and attempt to make the same payment after two weeks. Continue to pay the initial amount each month until you complete it.

This tactic is best used when you get paid after every two weeks because you can pay as soon as you receive money in your account. If you don't get paid after two weeks, try to set aside enough time from each paycheck to complete the two minimum payments each month.

As you make efforts to clear your credit card debt, you need to work to avoid accumulating more. Evaluate your expenses, create a budget for yourself, and stick to it. If possible, train yourself to pay using cash until the time when you know you can handle the bills on your credit card each month.

If you have ever been taken to the hospital, you are aware that medical charges can increase your credit card very fast. It is difficult to avoid medical bills because you also want to be treated. The first step you need to do with your medical bills is to check them for any errors. Ensure that you use all the services that you are getting charged for.

Apart from looking for errors and disclosing it to the hospital, you can still try to negotiate the medical bills.

Mortgage

Whether you applied for a mortgage in the last few days or have been paying off one for years, there are methods that you can try to cut it down and save money. Putting some effort into clearing your mortgage in advance is a great motivation because you'll increase both your security and the security of your family. In addition, you will be able to set aside some money to clear other debts. This way, you will increase your savings.

How you can reduce your mortgage

If you feel like your home mortgage is overwhelming, and you want to reduce the monthly payment, below are four methods that you can adopt:

1) Refinance the mortgage

Is it right to refinance? It depends on the period of the loan and the interval between the latest and expected interest rate.

"Home loans amortize"—this means the interest is paid at the start of the loan period, while the principal is paid at the end.

For that reason, the rate of interest is critical at the start of every period. In other words, the interest rate is of little importance at the end of the term when the principal is the primary payment. This means that for a new mortgage, you need to consider refinancing.

However, refinancing consumes a few thousand dollars in closing expenses. Thus, there will be little difference between the old and new interest rates.

2) Reduce your PMI

Do you have a private mortgage? If you purchased a home using a deposit that is lower than 20%, you could be paying PMI. This one adds hundreds of dollars to the mortgage at the end of each year.

There's some great news—you will not pay PMI forever. The first thing is to pay back enough of the mortgage that you receive 20% equity. Additionally, you can receive your stake earlier when the value of your home increases.

Next, get in touch with your lender and find out about the process of reducing the PMI. Lenders will not lessen the PMI automatically; that is why you need to ask for it. Most creditors will send an appraiser to define the property value to the creditor as verification that you have received 20% equity.

3) Select a longer loan

When you experience the pains of extreme monthly costs that have a 15-20-year mortgage, you can instead extend the mortgage into the traditional 30-year period to reduce your monthly expense.

The bad thing is that your interest rate will increase. The good thing is that you can decide to make an extra payment on the mortgage like you were paying for a 15-20-year loan. These additional payments will assist you in fulfilling the loan faster, without any mandate to make an extensive payment—let's say there is a crisis that causes you to be "cash-shy" for one or two months.

4) Challenge the tax evaluation

This is an unusual method to reduce your monthly payment. A traditional mortgage expense contains your principal amount, interest, and the "impounds", which can be a monthly expense the lender places on the assets taxes and the insurance of the homeowner.

So, if you refuse to pay the mortgage, the county can place a lien on your assets. A lien of the government will prioritize the lender's claim.

For that reason, the lender can pick the property taxes every month to secure the interest in your property. This payment is held in an escrow until the time when the yearly property tax bill will arrive. The property tax depends on the county's tax evaluation of the amount the home and land is worth.

Most of these evaluations are higher, especially during the home crash, which reduced home values. In some cases, the evaluation is higher when the region is rezoned. The new zoning will cause the property prices to reduce, and the reduced prices will not be reflected in the evaluation.

It is important to make appropriate plans to complete your mortgage on time. Any time you receive a rise on your income, consider channeling it into your debts.

Student loans

Education is another form of debt that has become more and more popular among young people. That said, there are many ways to cut down your student loans compared to other types of debt. This includes choosing to volunteer as a means of exchange for student loans. You can even apply the "Education Department's repayment" approximation tool to know the time it may take to be free from a student loan.

If you can plan, you can avoid future student loan debt. Here are some ways that you can adapt to reduce your student loans:

- Scholarships: These are given depending on the individual financial need, or sometimes, academic success. Even if you get a few awards that pay you a few small amounts, that is still progress in reducing your student debt.
- Grants: These are the same as scholarships, though they are given through organizations or the government.
- Work-study programs.
- Build a passive source of income so that you at least pay for some percentage of your student loan.
- Attempt income-based payment: If you get sizeable earnings, you can qualify for the income-based payment plan.

Student loans can be quite challenging because you will not know what you are going to receive when you apply for them. However, you can use some of the tactics mentioned to save more and repay your student loans.

Getting out of Debt

To assist you in attaining your financial freedom, the following is a step-by-step guide that will ensure you develop a debt pay-off plan and thus reduce your debt. Whether you have no money or your income is low, you can still adopt the following step-by-step debt guide to eliminate all your bills.

Let's go through the steps and assist you in getting out of debt for good.

Step 1: Determine the amount of debt you owe

It is impossible to develop a debt payment plan when you don't know how much money you need to pay back. It is critical that you know exactly what you're targeting. This is the time to mentally sum up all your debts from that $20 credit card balance to your $20,000 car loans, and compile everything into one.

Write down all the debts that you have, how much you need to pay, the rate of interest, and the minimum payment.

If you are not sure about your interest rate, spend some time opening your accounts and looking for the exact number. A high-interest debt rate is a massive drag on your achievements than a lower interest debt, so you need to learn which is which.

Adding everything in black and white can be quite scary, but you'll be preparing to reduce that number.

Step 2: Select your strategy: Debt Avalanche vs. Debt Snowball

Once you know how much you need to pay, it's time to come up with an action plan for how you are going to pay off all your debts.

By choosing to pay a little amount of money on every debt at the end of the month, without monitoring, is a surefire way to lose hope. It won't take long before you give up.

The right way to pay down debt is to concentrate on a single debt each time until that debt is fully paid. For now, pay small amounts on the remaining debts.

This will provide you with milestones to look back and celebrate; it will motivate you to keep going and make sure that you are organized for the whole period.

But the question is: how can you choose the first debt to start with?

There are two strategies when you want to decide; the "Debt Snowball Method" and the "Debt Avalanche Method".

Debt Snowball Strategy

If you can recall when you used to play snowball in the courtyard as a child, then you possibly learned that the quickest method to find traction was to put snow into a tight ball and begin to roll it in the yard. As it starts to acquire momentum and speed, the snowball starts to look like a snow boulder.

This is a great technique for creating snowballs, and it's even an effective way of clearing all your non-mortgage debt.

That is why it is called the debt snowball method. This method begins when you are at the Baby stage 2. During this stage, you are up-to-date on all your bills, and you have about $1,000 in first-course emergency funds saved. It is possibly a significant turning point in your whole money making process.

So, how does the debt snowball method work?

This method will help you reduce your debt. It involves paying off your debt, starting with the lowest to largest, and gaining momentum as you continue to reduce your balance. Once you complete paying the smallest debt, you can then roll the money for paying debt into the lowest balance.

It resembles something like this:

1. Organize your debts starting from the smallest to largest without considering the interest rate.
2. Pay a small amount on all your debts except the least amount.
3. Now, pay as much as you can on the least amount.
4. Repeat the process until you clear all your balances.

When using the snowball method, pay all the minimum payments except the medical bill—let's assume that you make some additional

$500 every month because you have a part-time job and you reduce your expenses to the minimum amount possible.

Why will this method work?

This strategy is related to behavior modification, but not the math involved. When it's narrowed down, hope has more to do with the equation than math. This means that if you start paying your student debt because it is the most significant debt, you will not clear it immediately. You'll see your balance reducing, but soon, you will lose the momentum because it will appear like you are taking a long time to pay. Apart from this, you will have other small amounts to pay.

The reason why it is called a debt snowball is due to the amount you strive to pay to clear your balance each month—you keep paying the same amount until your debts are cleared.

Debt Avalanche method

In a nutshell, this method requires you to prioritize the most significant interest rate to the lowest, but you ignore the size.

The procedure of the debt avalanche is the same as the debt snowball, except that with the following method, you plan to reduce the interest costs. There are no additional profits for the greedy creditors.

With this particular method, you begin by paying off the debt with the most substantial interest rate, no matter the size of the debt. Then you can move on to the next debt with the largest interest rate.

Why choose avalanche rather than snowball? The reason lies in removing high-interest costs. First, you will place most of your money towards the initial principal over time—in other words, you will get out of debt faster.

Choose which debt to deal with first

The most important thing is to get those quick early wins by paying small debts, or even the least amount of interest.

Both of the debts methods have their advantages. Even though the debt snowball isn't the cheapest way of paying the debt, it is effective. Aiming for a debt-free life can be a hard process, based on where you are starting from, and paying off some debts early on can quickly make you happy to continue paying.

Step 3: Make some huge changes

Though small, day-to-day changes are essential, some big changes can push you to clear your debt. Pay attention to the following ideas and decide whether the expense they represent is important to you.

Eliminate credit cards

Are credit cards generating a huge debt for you? It could be time to put an end to them.

If a credit card debt is a big problem, shift to cash and debit cards that can change your spending. Nothing is more painful than paying off debt when you know you increased it accidentally using impulse credit card buying.

After you are free from any debt, you can return to the matter. For the time being, credit card rewards can't remove your interest charges.

Sell your car

When you have a huge car payment, you need to opt for a cheaper model to reduce the debt and insurance costs.

Search for great car deals beyond the new car dealerships. You will get more opportunities to see private sales. However, be sure you have a professional mechanic to check the car before you purchase it.

If you don't have a car payment, you can choose whether your family requires one car or two. Taking your spouse to work each morning may appear like a big hassle, but if the extra 20 minutes can save you $600 a month, it could be worth it.

Stop investing

Saving for the future is important, but when you have a massive debt that is preventing you, then you will need to set your priorities. If you stop to invest temporarily, it can place you in a much better state to invest well in the future. Consider every dollar you save in interest costs like a dollar that is wisely invested.

However, it is not advisable to reduce your 400k to a point where you don't get the full employer match. That is free money, and the immediate return is higher than what you are paying as interest.

Sell unused possessions

We can all do with reducing stuff. But instead of throwing unused items in the dumpster, you can list them for sale on Craigslist, Facebook, or even LetGo.

On average, people have more than $1,000 worth of items that they don't use in their house. The small advantage of this process is that you will learn how many things you had bought for a higher amount of cash when you didn't need them. By realizing this, you can say no to spending unnecessarily in the future.

Cut cable

We are in 2019. Most of your favorite shows are online, and so it has become even easier to watch them. Now, if you haven't yet cut the cord, it's time to do so. The conventional cable packages cost more than $100 per month and can drag you down financially.

Step 4: Build a monthly budget

If you want to know the amount of money you need to set aside each month to pay your debts, then you need to have a budget. A reasonable budget will help you to track where your money is going. It will alert you where the money is not being used properly. It will also alert you to how much you can afford for the things that you want.

By creating a budget and giving yourself some flexibility, you will learn how to manage stress by understanding that there is always money in the bank for the things that you want.

How you can control your budget

Before you start, keep in mind that the budget you develop today is bound to change with time. Your spending habits and categories will change in the first few months. And that is fine. You will need some time to adjust to monitoring your expenses and remaining aware of your needs.

How to create a budget by following five easy steps

1. Determine the amount of money you make

Find out how much you are paid per period. This is what you are going to work with.

2. Determine your main expenses

Groceries, housing, insurance, and utilities. These are non-negotiable costs that need to be covered first.

3. Write down your debt payments

For the time being, let's assume that you only make a minimum payment on all your debts because that is the amount needed.

4. Build categories for regular expenses and allocate reasonable price limits for every item

Don't be scared to have many budget categories. This will assist you in understanding how things run. Some ordinary expenses include household products, cell phone, medical costs, car repair, and home repair. Keep in mind that not every product will have a cost each month, but if you can set some money aside for the irregular expenses, you'll be prepared when the time comes.

5. Assign the remaining cash between debt pay down and quality of life expenses

The money left from your income after you have completed Step 2 – Step 4 is the amount of money that you have raised towards your goals and fun. Plus, you might want to allow room for gifts, dinners out, gym membership, and many more. Divide the cash in a manner that works for you.

Although you may want to manage your goals fast, remember to set aside some pocket money. Even if it is only going to pay for a single Starbuck coffee every month, these little treats will keep you motivated.

If you have some money left after Step 4, you might have to assess your core and regular expenses. Without massive changes in lifestyle, you can be stuck and experience a huge problem to get out of debt.

As you get used to the budget, don't be scared to transfer money from one side to another. There is never such a thing as a normal month. Don't overspend and completely go off track because of failing to predict the cost of a house repair accurately.

Use Trim to reduce your monthly bills

If you want to reduce your bills without negotiating with a company, then Trim is the best tool to use.

Trim is a useful money-saving tool. The free app will send you updates on how much you are spending through text and look for unwanted subscriptions—and cancel them for you—at the same time. You can negotiate your internet bill.

Step 5: Reduce your interest rates to save money

The lower the amount of interest you pay your creditors, the faster you will avoid your debt. Read on to learn how you can decrease your interest rates.

Refinancing student loans

If the student loans are pulling you back, you can decide to refinance to a much lower rate for a shorter period.

By lowering the term of your loans, a lower interest rate will possibly raise your monthly payment. However, with fewer years of payment, you can manage to save a bundle.

Bargain for your credit card interest rates

Remember that credit card interest rates aren't fixed. The market is very competitive for the credit card company, which means that they need to be flexible to retain customers.

If you're a long-time customer and have a better standing, you can call and request for an interest reduction. In most cases, they will be ready to reduce the cut and hold you as a customer.

Some of the things to let them know so that they can listen to you is to tell them the period that you have been a loyal customer and that you would like to continue being loyal. However, at the same time, let them know that other credit card companies are providing a lower interest rate, which could be 0% introductory rates for the balance transfers. They will probably accept your request.

Make plans for a balance transfer credit card

If you can't reduce your interest rates, you should make plans for a balance transfer, which will allow you to transfer debt from one credit card to a different card using a lower rate—sometimes even 0%.

Effectively, you will be paying off a single credit card using another. However, when the difference in rate is wide enough, that could save you money. Just ensure that you have all the details before you begin a transfer. Most balance transfer cards charge a fee of 3%-5%. Also, there could be limits on the amount that one can transfer.

Although 0% interest appears fantastic, only choose a balance transfer when you are sure about paying the debt. Ensure that you can clear the balance during the 0% period. If not, you will be playing around with your balance.

Step 6: Change your spending habits

You need to acknowledge a frugal mindset so that you can limit your spending and effectively chase your goals. If you aren't sure where to start from, you can begin with the big stuff.

Save money on food every month

The average American is said to spend about 10% of their budget on food, one of the highest after housing. It is important to eat, but again, we pay a lot for it. Here's how you can reduce your expenditure on food:

Stop eating out

Not only is eating at a restaurant very expensive, but it is also risky for your waistline. The meals served at a restaurant are quite expensive and more than the average dinner prepared at home.

More than 4% of the American budget is spent on outside food. If you purge out dining from your budget, at least until you have no debt, it could be helpful.

Avoid impulse buying

Before a trip to your weekly grocery store, spend some time to create a list. Look at your grocery store's online circular and use the Ibotta app to see what is put on sale. From here, you can come up with a meal plan and list your items.

Once you step inside the grocery store, make sure to stick to your list. To limit any additional purchases that are triggered by hunger, make sure that you take some snacks before going to the store.

Learn to say "NO."

Going shopping and drinking with your friends are very tempting. However, when these things are included in your spendings, you're sacrificing your future for a little fun today.

Don't be scared to say "no" to any event that you can't manage—no need to isolate yourself on your journey to become debt free though. Simply be ready to offer a different option. You can recommend a game night at your place, and this would mean more quality time with your friends for less money.

Let go of your expensive hobbies

If you spend $100 per month on yoga lessons, that is not realistic when you are aiming to pay off your debts. This is the time when you need to give up your costly hobbies, or even seek lower cost hobbies, such as a monthly book club.

Step 7: Increase the level of income

Frugal living is great, but there are limits. It is hard to save more than what you can earn. For you to take your debt-free journey to another level, it is high time that you generate some extra dough.

Request a pay rise

If you know that you have been working hard and providing value to your company, it's not bad to request a raise.

Don't just drop the request in your employer's lap. Request for feedback, build your skills and take on more responsibility. Along the way, you can proactively allow your superiors to know what they have achieved. You want your manager to realize that you need a raise before you even walk through the door.

Begin a side hustle

If you know you can get some spare time, commit it to doing something that you enjoy or love to earn some money. Since the average person spends five hours watching TV every day, you can be sure to get that time. You can even start today by signing up for online sites such as Survey Junkie, or even review websites using User Testing.

Begin a low-overhead online business

The internet has simplified many things; for example, you can start a business with zero up-front costs. Set up an online shop as a freelance writer, virtual assistant, and proofreader and provide your services to companies that want to outsource their work. You can work for as many hours as you want, with some people turning their business into a six-figure job.

Look for clients by calling local businesses, post your new business on LinkedIn, or even list your services on Upwork.

Compiling everything

Whether you are breaking down or don't have money, it is important to stick to the above steps to become debt free for good.

Once you have an action plan for how you can get out of debt, attaining debt freedom requires patience. Remain focused on your goal, stick to your budget, reduce the fat from your spending, and look for means to generate more income to speed up the whole process.

Three helpful tips to clear your credit card debt

Having a healthy financial habit will allow you to sleep comfortably and enjoy your sleep.

If you have ever woken up while sleeping at night and trembled because of the amount of debt you have to pay, you aren't alone. Credit card debt is the second most popular type of debt after the mortgage debt. The average American family has a credit card debt of about $8,377. This is according to the personal finance site WalletHub, which analyzed credit card debt in 2016.

As a reminder, debt can be good or bad. Good debt is one that you can use to win more assets. Bad debt is one that pulls you back instead of moving you forward. In most instances, credit card debt is a form of bad debt. That is the reason why you need to eliminate it—

it's not doing any good in your life. Below are some recommendations for reducing your credit card debt once and for all:

1. Clear your credit card fees each month

Credit cards have an advantage too so you should not destroy them or throw them in the freezer. Instead, you need to use them as a convenience, a record-monitoring tool, and as a means to confirm other creditors and the ability to be responsible financially.

From today, henceforth, avoid accumulating extra credit card debt. If you purchase an item using your credit card, make sure to clear that amount when presented with the statement. If your credit card debt is more than 30 days, then you should pay off all the debt and create a plan to pay off the credit card debt.

The credit card interest often compounds. For example, let's say you have a $200 debt and it accrues 20% interest per month. In the first month, you will be hit with $40, which is added to your original debt. In the following month, you will be charged 20%, which comes to $48. In other words, after two months, your debt will rise from $200 to $288. That is just throwing money away, and nobody can afford to do that.

2. Avoid charging the small stuff

It is quite surprising how fast our small purchases increase. And it is now easy to verify all the small purchases. $3 for a lip balm—just because you forgot yours at home—may appear small, but at the end of the month, each purchase will add up.

Using physical paper money will build awareness of how much you are wasting every day. This should make you think about the small purchases when you discover that you are running out of cash fast. So starting today, try to buy items under $20 and see how your spending habits change.

How to eliminate debt and become rich in 2019

To be debt free and get richer is easier said than done.

About half of households in the US have a credit card debt, and the average amount of that debt is over $8,000. For many people, that is a huge amount, but the good thing is that it's not.

It is not a surprise that many people start the New Year with resolutions to pay off all their debts, but the primary challenge is that they do not come up with the right strategy to help them come out of debt. Even worse is that they don't have the financial smartness to know what they need to do with the amount of money they save from avoiding to pay the debt. Finally, bad habits come back, and before they realize it, they are already trapped in a credit card debt.

That means it is not enough to avoid bad credit card debt, but it is crucial to develop a plan for the money to help you rise to riches. In this section, we present to you Rich Dad-SIX POINT PLAN to get out of debt and become rich in 2019.

Tip 1: If you have credit cards with existing balances, have one or two credit cards in your wallet.

You have perhaps seen individuals in line whose card is rejected only for them to flush out another card from their wallet or purse. You don't want to be this person anymore, and the right way to avoid being this person is to prevent the temptation.

So, purposely carry only one or two cards. Keep other cards out of sight, preferably in a safe. For any new changes that occur to the one or two cards in your possession, make sure you pay the charges every month. Avoid getting into long-term bad debt.

Tip 2: Make an extra $150-$200 per month.

When you face a harsh economic environment, learn how to hustle. Look for some odd jobs while you plan on starting your own business. It is not hard to earn a small amount of cash as long as you keep your mind open to opportunities around you. If you can't generate $150-$200 per month, then your probabilities of attaining financial freedom may be very limited.

For most people, this could be as simple as evaluating your monthly expenses and identifying areas where you can stop spending on items that aren't necessary. Avoid eating out. Avoid buying more clothes than you need and paying for online services you rarely use. As you can see, there are many opportunities to exploit if you want to save that extra $200.

However, if you want to extend your ability and increase your financial ability, look for means to generate an extra $200 per month. It is easy to reduce the given expenses; however, teaching yourself how to make money will be more satisfying in the long run.

Tip 3: Use the additional $150-$200 on your monthly payment for just one of your credit cards.

Look for the minimum card balance, and then pay the lowest plus the extra cash on that one credit card. Why? Because the rule of the game is to reduce your monthly payments on a bad debt. You possibly have a lower balance card, which, when it is paid off, will save you a ton of money every month.

Once you pay the minimum card balance plus the additional $150-$200, pay the least amount due on all other credit cards. In most cases, people want to pay some extra amount every month on each credit card that they own, but surprisingly, those cards never get paid.

Tip 4: Once you finish with the first card, apply the whole amount you have been paying on that card to the next credit card.

Pay the least amount on the second card plus the sum of the monthly payment you were paying for the first credit card.

Keep up with this process for all your credit cards plus consumer credit. For every debt that you complete, add the total amount that you were paying on the previous card to the minimum payment of your next debt. As you continue to clear your debt, the monthly amount that you were previously paying will rise.

Tip 5: Once you finish with your credit cards, apply the same to your house and car payments.

This is the part about getting rich. The fact is: the worst debt you clear, the richer you become. In other words, little money is coming from your pocket and going into making banks and creditors rich. However, the real magic of this strategy originates from taking the money you were using to pay your debts and channeling it into investments that generate cash every month. So the money that you used to lose each month will be making more money for you. And that is pretty cool.

The good thing is that you don't have to do this alone. You can involve friends and experts who can advise you on each step. There is great power in the community.

It is possible to become debt free and rise to riches. However, you need to make that decision first and be ready to implement each step. Remain focused on your goal, and look for ways to make more money and speed up your journey to becoming rich. Don't forget to celebrate every milestone that you make too—this will help you to keep up with the spirit!

Chapter 3: Budgeting for Beginners

A budget gives you freedom. It is the path to learning what is most important. Many people find it difficult to arrange a trip to a new place with loved ones, or even go out and enjoy themselves. But this is the result when we waste our hard earned cash on unnecessary expenditures. A budget can help you realize your goals in life.

Now, if you are among the millions of people who are in debt or depend on a paycheck, those qualities add a specific layer to the budget, but a reasonable budget is crucial to consumers with the least financial resources than anyone else. However, the budget is still your tool to come out of a chaotic and indebted life.

Let's see:

What is your monthly income?

The first thing that you need to do is to determine the amount of money that you earn every month. Add everything up, including child support, wages, and other forms of income.

The amount of money that you earn is important because it reflects the amount that you will work with every month. You can't afford to spend more than this number, or you'll increase your debt.

List down your expenses

The next thing is to write down your necessary expenses. These are the types of bills that you will need to pay every month. It can include rent, property taxes, cell phone, average utilities, car payment, child support, groceries, insurance, and medications.

Spotify, Cable TV, and other things should not be on this list. In this section, you will need to concentrate on "must-have expenses". These are things that you will need to pay so that you can prevent creditors from being on your toes.

Analyze the spending

It is crucial that you build a realistic budget. You may want to spend $50 every month dining out, but if your usual expenditure is $800 per month, what's the probability that a $50 monthly budget is going to work for you? There is a good chance that after two weeks, you will have given up.

That is why you need to review your spending patterns and see how you can begin with the current budget. Along the way, you can then start to scale it. You may have to recheck your bank transactions or credit card statements. If you use cash, you will need to look for receipts or maintain a daily log for about two weeks, and perhaps, a whole month.

Write down your non-essential expenses

Now that you have some knowledge about how you spend compile a list of all your non-essential expenses. We aren't making judgments or cuts at all; you need to create a list. Some of the categories that you may want to consider are:

- Gym fees
- Pet expenses
- Dining out
- Entertainment

- Clothing
- Toiletries
- Fuel
- Health expenses

Now it is time to sum your budget

In this section, you will see how an actual budget is created. This is merely a list of categories with some cash assigned to every amount. You can refer to it as a spending plan as that is the accurate description of what it does.

First, look for a piece of paper, a software program, or spreadsheet, and write your total income plus your must-have expenses—this should contain the approximate amount of money that is channeled to each category. It may resemble the following example:

- Income for May – $4,000
- Rent – $995
- Gas – $50
- Credit card – $75
- Electricity – $100
- Groceries – $500
- Student Loans – $370

Next, list down your unnecessary expenses, and make sure you factor in your current spending characteristics.

This is the part where you can challenge yourself. Look at the numbers and see whether you have any that can be scaled. For example, if you always spend $500 per month on groceries, can you commit to shopping sales and reduce the amount to $450?

If you think you can reduce the spending in certain areas, then you should proceed and write down the new number.

Your remaining budget may appear this way:

- Pets – $10
- Restaurants – $150
- Fun money – $100
- Netflix – $10
- Hair appointment – $60

Once you list everything down, add all the expenses. The total amount you get will reflect the amount of money you spend. Determine whether it is less than your income. If not, you will have to look for more places to reduce your spending.

How much should remain?

Financial experts advise that a person have a 20% buffer to go to savings or pay the debt. This means if you earn $5,000 per month, you need to ensure you are left with $1,000 to redirect that to savings or even reduce your debt. This could be a difficult goal, especially when you depend on a paycheck, but it is worth it to try.

What if you don't have a buffer?

Well, you will need to ensure that you spend less than what you get if you want to make any savings or cut down the paycheck-to-paycheck cycle. If you are going to spend more than what you earn every month, then you will have destroyed the plan. If this is the kind of situation that you are going through, you have two things to do: you can decide to look for more ways to make extra income, or you need to reduce your cost. You can try both.

It is possible to get a job, and then do some side jobs to boost your earnings. Alternatively, you can ask for a pay rise, sell some items, or even think about switching jobs—if the one you have isn't the best option.

Spend time analyzing your monthly expenses. Do you *really* need Netflix? Is it possible to spend less on food by either limiting the number of times you dine out or go to the grocery store? Can you look for a roommate or relocate to new housing? Each of your expenses requires in-depth analysis. Ask yourself whether you are ready to give up this expense and change your financial situation.

Set an emergency fund

Let's ensure that you eliminate any chances of running into debt in the future. One way that you can do this is by having an emergency savings account. One thing that you must know is that emergencies are bound to occur, and perhaps when you least expect them.

If you have a nice sum of cash set aside for these events, then you will manage to overcome the challenge without any trouble. If you don't have an emergency fund, you are probably risking yourself, especially when an emergency strikes.

Set aside an emergency fund before you begin to pay your debt. Begin with enough money to cover your costs. Set aside some cash each month in savings until you have your emergency fund set aside. Implement an automatic transfer so that it becomes easy to save.

The best place to store your emergency savings account is on an interest-earning savings account so that you can earn some interest as you save. It can't be much, but the right savings rate should be approximately 1%. You can try out Credit Sesame account to identify the best savings account for you. Once you sign in, you can hover your mouse around the "Loans" tab at the top of the page and click the "Banking" button to read the latest recommendations.

Analyze the debt

Many people have the perception that the payment of debt is a fixed expense. That is correct, but you can shape it to fit your budget better, or even pay it off early so that you don't need to worry about paying debts.

The first thing is to assess your debt. You can navigate to Credit Sesame profile. You will see a section on your right screen called "MY DEBT ANALYSIS". Click on the "VIEW DETAILS" button at the bottom of the box. The picture below shows the way the screen looks:

Are your debts typed correctly?

You will navigate to a page that will list all your debts. It is crucial to cross-check to ensure every debt is entered correctly, and that no debt is left out. You don't want to see surprises on this page—if so, you could be a victim of identity fraud.

Is your debt-to-income ratio very low?

Your debt-to-income ratio is the percentage measure of your monthly income, and what is directed to the debt payments. Lenders love to see a low debt-to-income ratio. How are they sure that they are going to receive their money when you have already planned to spend it elsewhere?

Overall, a lower debt ratio is much better, and the best debt-to-income ratio would be zero—meaning no debt. It can be terrifying to see the percentage of your income that is channeled to the payment of debts, but this should not worry you, especially when you have no problem with it. In the next section, you will see a plan to use to pay it off.

Do you have a credit utilization that is below 10%?

Lenders also want to see that you can manage your credit cards. They can notice this by looking at your credit card utilization ratio or the percentage of the available credit you are using. Many lenders want to see 10% credit utilization or even less. High usage can affect a healthy credit score.

To look for your usage ratio, you can click on the "My Credit button" located at the top of the screen. From here, you will be directed to a page that has different tabs. Click on the tab labeled "Credit Usage".

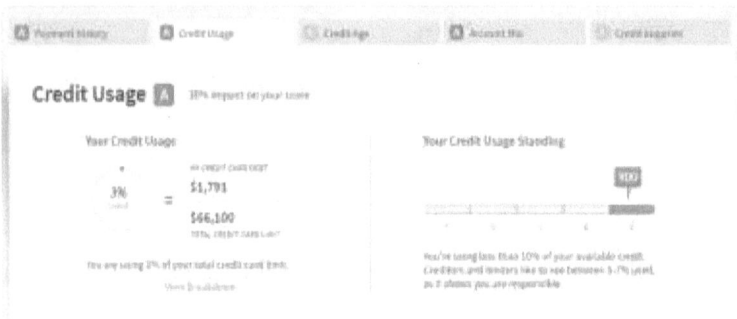

Now, if your usage is more than 10%, don't be scared. You will see a plan that you can implement to reduce it.

Is it right to pay off debt or save?

Money is usually tight, and it can be a bit challenging to pay off debt and save. However, you need to save your emergency fund first.

Once you have finished paying your debts, you can decide to save a larger emergency fund.

Customize your debt to fit your budget

Reduce the credit utilization ratio.

In case your credit utilization ratio is more than 10%, one of the most important things that you will first want to do is bring it down. Your credit usage ratio has a massive effect on your score, and if you can bring it down, it will be of significance in the long term because your credit score will increase and your debt will drop. In other words, you will manage to qualify for better rates and terms on credit cards and loans.

Identify your "Total Credit Limit" by clicking on the "Credit Usage tab". Divide that number by ten. That will be your target. So you need to pay most of your credit card debt to attain this number.

For instance, if you have a $10,000 total credit limit, the ideal figure of debt would be $1,000 or less. If you have a debt of $3,000 on your credit cards, focus on paying the first $2,000.

Analyze the refinance options

The correct method to lower the cost of debt both short term and long term is by refinancing the debt to a lower interest rate, and there are a few methods to do this. However, before you begin, ask yourself whether you want to reduce the monthly payments or want to be debt free.

You could manage to get a low monthly payment for your debt if you decide to refinance into a long-term loan, but for the entire period of this loan, you could pay more interest fees. On the other side, you can save and earn a lot of money to spend a considerable amount to pay your debt every month and stay free of that debt faster. It all depends on what you decide to do.

You can "refinance student loans" with private lenders, but you must know that if you have federal loans, you will lose most of the protections such as deferment, repayment plans, and forgiveness on student loan plans. The best option for federal student loans is to combine them into a single federal loan by applying an averaged-out interest rate. This may not save any money, but it will simplify your financial life.

All other forms of loans are a fair channel to refinance. It is possible to refinance your car, RV, mortgage, and anything else that you have loans for. The right tools for non-mortgage debt include personal loans. Fortunately, you can look at what personal loans you can receive by using Credit Sesame's tools.

Once you sign in, click the "Borrowing Power" tab found at the top of the screen and navigate down until you can see the

INSTALLMENT LOAN section. This part will feature information that you need to develop an informed refinancing decision.

Look for offers of credit card balance transfer

If you have a credit card debt, you can pay it faster with the help of the "zero-interest balance transfer card". To achieve this, you will have to apply for the new card, transfer the remaining credit card balance, and pay down the debt interest until the time when the zero percent APR expires.

You can look at what credit card transfer balance cards you are likely to be approved for by applying Credit Sesame's tools. Sign in to your account and navigate to the "My Recommendations" tab and scroll until you come across the 0% Intro APT offers.

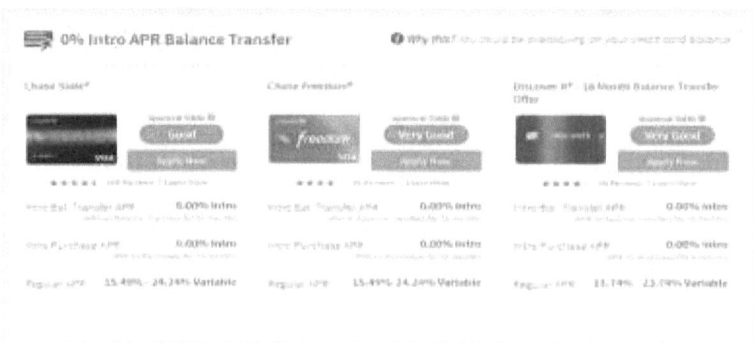

Select a debt payoff plan

Now is the time to choose a debt payoff plan; this is the time to get serious about paying your debt. You can either choose to use the debt snowball method or debt avalanche method.

Each of the above strategies depends on building a "hit-list" of the debts based on their level of priority. The debt snowball strategy prioritizes the minimum debt first so that you can receive quick wins. On the other hand, the debt avalanche focuses on the highest-interest-rate debt first because that is your highest debt.

Once you manage to clear your first debt based on the method you choose, you pick the monthly payment and use it in the next debt on your list. Continue repeating this process and increase your monthly payment on your target debt by a figure that is equivalent to the payment you made on the last debt.

Review your budget every month

Every month, you need to run an analysis of your budget. This will help you to know areas where you overspend or spend less. A budget is like a living document, and you can alternate your numbers around every month to make it work for you.

You can also run a quick analysis every month of your loan, refinancing, and balance transfer plan on your Credit Sesame dashboard. As you reduce your debt, your credit choices will increase. Additionally, the market changes every day, and the quotes you were told last may be lower than for this month.

As long as you stay updated with your budget and ensure that you are progressing and attaining your financial goals, you will soon be debt free.

Money-management for singles

Single people have no one to remind them what they can do, and no one can interfere with their plans. That sounds great. However, they also have the central challenge of having no accountability. As a result, things can get out of control very fast. According to Kiplinger's magazine, it was discovered that 30% of people who file for bankruptcy are women, while 26% are men. As you can see, this is a big deal.

A poll conducted by the "Pew Research Center" discovered that approximately 80% of 18-25-year-olds in the U.S consider being rich as the top goal in their life. Now here's a fact for you: you won't be rich if you consider debt as the tool to propel you to richness. It is vital that single people learn to practice the right financial skills like the way married people do.

Managed cash works harder

If you think you aren't making sufficient money to budget, then you have to think again. When you list your purpose/s for money, you are already making it. You are free to do whatever you want to do because you don't have a person that you need to be accountable to. However, you need to ask yourself, "Am I behaving in a manner that will help me attain my goals?" Being broke because you don't practice the correct money management practices is bad.

Look for a money mentor

Look for a person with experience and knowledge about financial matters. This should be a person who has a proven track record with money. Ask him or her lots of questions. Grant permission to this person to supervise your budget and review with them before you "spend big". This person has to like and respect you to the point where they aren't ashamed to hit you with the truth when you start to go wrong with your expenditure. Don't allow overconfidence to take control because it can make you avoid asking for any input from anyone.

Avoid impulse buying

For single parents, this tendency to buy things on impulse arises from immaturity instead of desperation. As a single parent with not enough money, you have one option, and that is to plan. You should know that you are trapped by certain situations you want to be free from and that require a plan to break.

Those who don't have children perhaps have a diverse type of impulsive streak. How many times in a week do you dine out? Do you go shopping every week at the mall? How much are you paying for your car?

Putting the right steps into practice will help you to explore more freedom. If you make the right decisions, you will achieve the benefits in the future.

Setting up a couple's budget

If you are living together as a couple, but not yet legally married, it is not a good move to compile finances into one. The reason is that you don't have the same security as legally married couples. As a result, your household budget should only deal with house expenses.

Until the time you are married, you need to have separate expenses to secure yourself in case you split up.

1. Determine the expenses that you want to share

First, you must decide the costs that you want to share in the house. In general, you may have to split the rent, basic groceries, and utilities. If there are pets in the house, include pet care in the budget.

As a couple, you need to agree on what should and shouldn't be part of the household budget. Have a small household emergency kit that has about $1,000 in it to handle unexpected expenses.

2. Define your contribution amount

Some people would recommend that each of you has to contribute an equal amount to the household expenses because you are living together. However, splitting costs isn't the right way to do it.

In general, one person usually earns more than the other, and 50% of the costs could freeze up all the money of the person earning little income. Contributing to the budget based on your income percentage is a great way to handle it. Also, it will provide you with the opportunity to save some cash for your retirement plan.

3. Estimate your amount of contribution

To find out the amount of money each of you needs to contribute, you have to compute the gross amounts and add up the household budget. Next, divide the gross pay by the household budget.

The percentage that you receive should be the percentage that each one of you needs to contribute. For instance, if you generate $6,000 per month, and your partner generates about $4,000, and the household budget is about $2,500 per month, then you will add $6,000 and $4,000.

4. Create a separate checking account

You need to sign up for a single checking account meant for your household costs.

Both of you need to sign the account and schedule a date where you can deposit into the account to handle the monthly bills.

From here, you can pay for the costs that belong to the household budget using the account. This will provide security to your money just in case your partner makes the wrong choices. Also, it makes things simple if a split occurs in the future.

Using this account to secure all your household expenses will restrict you from using a credit card or covering costs shared.

5. The products that you are responsible for

You need to be accountable enough to pay for your expenses. If you want to buy clothes, ensure you use your money. Additionally, you should pay 15% of your gross income into your retirement plan. Being completely responsible for loans and credit cards is important.

6. Creating a budget for the remaining income

It is important to set your budget to control your spending. This type of budget will assist you in tracking your retirement plan contributions and protecting you from getting into a wrong financial situation.

It is critical to follow the normal rules of budgeting while you develop the budget. However, ensure that you include the main aspects and items in the budget.

7. Keep the expenses separate

It is important to ensure that external expenses are not part of the household account. You should avoid buying things together because you aren't married; you are only de facto or engaged.

Buying a car or home together can cause breaking up to be hard. If you want to save money for a down payment when you are married, you should save separately and provide a report of the progress.

The moment you are married, it is important to examine your budget and include your expenses.

This will simplify everything in case you split up because of a job transfer. Also, it will assist you in concentrating on the weaknesses of the budget instead of looking at how your partner spends money.

Creating a family budget

With all the needs that come with having a family, it is difficult to get time to create a house budget, especially when you are left with the lowest amount of money. It is a good thing to factor in household expenses because that is the only method that you can control them— if not, they will control you.

The procedure of building a family budget requires time, so you need to allocate some hours for this, and a time where you can concentrate well enough to create a good budget.

Begin with a goal. It could be to clear your debt or even a college fund. There is no need to let everyone know your goal, but by imagining your goal, it will help you to remain on track.

Select the style of your budget

A pen and paper help you draft an accurate budget. However, using modern software makes the whole process simple. In addition, it will flag any potential errors that you can make.

If you think the paper is right for you, though, you may have to look for an accounting ledger; this one will not cost you much. In all languages, credits are referred to as the incoming cash and debits as the outgoing cash.

Electronic software tools for budget, such as Mint.com, are one of the most straightforward solutions to consider. There is no need to write everything; in-built software should generate running totals, send offers, and indicate the way debit and credit affect each other.

Bring everything to the table

Nearly everything that describes the flow of cash, such as the bills, bank statements, earning statements, and receipts, should have a place at the budget table. The first thing to do is divide them into types: incoming and outgoing.

You may require a sum for all the budget categories. This is the point where many budget creators become nervous. However, you don't need to be. The inbound amount could be lesser than the outgoing, but having a budget will allow you to regulate that.

Identify where your money goes

The outbound type requires much attention once you get the total. The next thing to do is break the debts into subcategories. Yours could be utilities, unsecured debts, discretionary spending, or unsecured debts.

Set up your ledger, spreadsheet, and any financial tools

When your first categories and totals are ready, you can sum everything using an electronic budget program. This is the point from which the budget starts to align in shape. Your primary goal should be to get the debits at a lower price than your credits.

Regulate the discretionary spending

At this point, it should be easy for one to approach the monthly budget in a manner that is realistic. A flexible means of spending could be the only option where you can look and divert the cash towards a debt reduction and saving.

The correct means to control your discretionary spending is to use the "envelope method". The money you assign for daily expenses is transferred to the envelope every month. With real cash in hand, you tend to be more aware and reduce the probability of overspending.

Pay off the debt

The reduction of debt is the primary goal of many families. The only means to reach this is to pay some minimum amount of money every month. If you spend more than the minimum amount, it will quickly decrease your debt.

Confirm with the creditor so that you can be sure every additional payment will go the way you want. Sometimes, interest can be a fixed amount that will not change, no matter how much you pay every month.

Budgeting can be both simple and challenging. You merely need to know how much you make, and what you need to pay as debt, and at which point money is spent. The reason why it is complex is that it is challenging to know where to cut back and which point to channel more money. For certain families, debt could be the main problem. Without the required resources, debt can accumulate, and the credit scores can be crippled.

When there is a higher payment than what you can manage, and you can't get any additional income, a free credit counseling service such as the National Foundation for Credit Counseling can be helpful.

A reasonable budget can assist you in fulfilling your financial goals for the family.

Building a personal budget plan using irregular income

If you have a student loan or you depend on a commission to make money, you could be tired of the advice of budgeting to save money.

If your income keeps changing, or you rely on a large sum of money to support you through different times of the month, then it could be hard to come up with a budget.

Get started with a budget – how you can plan for expenses

Before you dive in to try any of the following strategies, spend some time highlighting your expenses. Write down your commitments.

Then, you can add the amount for the lower expenses you require to spend money on. These can be difficult to identify than regular costs, so you need to look through your calendar and credit card statements and begin to reconstruct your spending habits.

When your income is irregular, fluctuates, or seasonal, concentrate on planning and adopting a budget and money management method that will prevent your spending from being uneven.

Below are three personal budgeting and money management strategies to get you started:

1. Create the budget using average income

If your income has been irregular for some years, one method is to determine your annual average net income for the last three years and divide it by twelve. The amount you get, channel it to your current monthly budget. When the amount is insufficient to fulfill all your costs, you should look for ways to increase your income amount consistently to balance your budget. For those who are self-employed, the planning process for any budget method should have a savings account.

2. Develop two kinds of budgets

In this particular method, you will run two types of budgets. The first budget is meant for good times, and the other budget is to help you during the worst days. However, note that this method can be challenging to use to manage finances because of the temptation to overspend.

When there are two kinds of budget, some people may be tempted to use money unnecessarily because they know that they will make more during the best times. They rely on credit to facilitate their expenditure in the tough times, and this may create a cycle of debts.

3. Budget with the help of a holding account

This method is appropriate for students. Your entire income amount is placed on a holding account. Next, you can start to pay a portion of your monthly income based on what you can control and what will allow you to attain your obligations. When your income is high, the holding account will have a large balance. In harsh times, your balance will drop. However, the amount you pay every month doesn't change.

N/B

This method should be the easiest for post-secondary students that budget with a lot of money. With grants and bursaries saved from working in the summer, it can be easy to spend it.

A personal budget will allow you to concentrate on what you can do instead of what you can't, even when your income is irregular. Spending time building a realistic budget will simplify your life because you will now be able to manage your money.

Reasons why you need to stick to your budget

Creating a budget is one of those principles in personal finance that anyone who wants to save money has to focus on. It is learning how to live within your means that can help you know how to save. But why is it important to live according to your budget? Though most people know that sticking to your budget can help them save money, there are plenty of other reasons:

1. So that you can give your money time to appreciate

If you have never developed a budget, you may be afraid to build one, but don't be scared. Many people look at a budget as a means to restrict their life, but that is not the truth. In fact, the opposite is what is true. If you ever wanted to experience financial freedom, then a budget is the tool that will help you realize your goal. Have you ever taken the time to look at your bank account at the end of the month and wondered where your money goes? If you can teach yourself how to set attainable expenses every month, it will grant you the freedom to do other things with your income.

2. You need to save for your goals

The first thing that you must know is the amount you are going to generate after you remove your tax. From here, you can move on to decide your expenses. The "50/30/20" budget is very common. It will provide "50%" of the after-tax income to be spent on the relevant expenses, such as transportation, housing, and utilities.

The "30%" of your income has to be placed to deal with the long-term goals, such as purchasing a home. The remaining "20%" of the income can be saved to assist in short-term goals like a yearly vacation and emergency savings fund.

3. Learn to live within your means

How can you get started? The first thing is to monitor your spending to determine whether you are following the 50/30/20 budget style. If you aren't, you will need to identify unnecessary expenses that you can deduct from your income. Use a budget software app to help you monitor your spending for the next 30 days. From this point, you can reassign your spending and ensure that your monthly bills are paid. Also, you need to make sure that you are saving towards your goals.

4. To avoid any debt

Not only will a budget help you to live within your means, but it will also assist you in avoiding getting into unnecessary debt. You will be able to spend according to what you have set out in the budget. In other words, you won't find yourself entering into any debt without a plan. Creating a budget and sticking to it will assist you in avoiding entering into debt, and it will assist you in paying off your current debt.

5. To build a good credit history

If you want to have a good credit history, then sticking to a budget is the sure way to create a nice credit history. Determine your monthly debt payments into your must-have expenses. This one will offer you the ability to spend within a budget and pay all your balance in full at the end of every month. Also, it will assist you in avoiding debt and unnecessary interest charges.

6. You want to avoid living the "rat race"

We all want to stop working at one point in our lives. That can only happen when we begin to save money for retirement and avoid laying our hands on the money until we are prepared to part ways with the working world. Ensure that you assign a certain amount of your long-term goals budget to your retirement account so that your dream can come true.

Nobody wants to view a budget as something restrictive, but it is the best way to monitor your money as you enter into the world of personal finance. Each lifestyle and budget of everyone is different. And this is what makes personal finance "personal". So build your budget based on the amount of money you earn, goals, and needs in life.

Five motivations to help you live according to your budget

Sticking to a budget that you create is not an easy thing, but it comes with many benefits, as mentioned previously.

Directing your money where it should go every month provides you with a feeling of total control and assists you in planning for the future. Regardless of your financial dream, a budget is the primary step to reaching it. It will allow you to develop an effective plan for how you use your money and set priorities.

However, this doesn't mean that you deny yourself all the things that drive happiness in your life. If you want to go out and enjoy some drinks with your friends every month, or even get a massage, that's still fine. As long as you are responsible and disciplined with your budget, such that the above things don't interfere with your monthly expenses, why not? Creating a budget will give you the financial freedom to enjoy the money that you make without getting worried about it because you have set a plan for it.

But sticking to the plan can be easier said than done. You can be tempted to use your vacation savings to purchase the latest smartphone. The "I want" part of your brain can persuade you, but there are some things that you can do to stick to a budget, even when you feel weak to do so:

Look for someone who will be accountable for you

It is important that you get a person who is in the same condition as you when setting your budget. This could be a family member or spouse. Or you can have a weekly budget review with a friend through Facebook. Show your goals, run the figures, and accept where you have gone wrong. Getting support and encouragement will help you to stay on track and focus.

Be realistic

If you want to scale certain parts of your budget so that you can pay down debt or even save for a future vacation, that is good for you. However, it is vital to ensure that your budget is realistic. Don't scale down your groceries to the point where you are eating rice and beans every day or even abandon your whole entertainment budget and resort to living as a hermit.

Keep in mind that a little fun will ensure that you remain resilient enough to follow your budget. When you start to feel like you lack something, this can easily render you into a state of rebellion. Scale down within reason, but don't eliminate everything.

Set a no-spend day

When you spend a little here and there, you may think that you aren't spending a lot. However, after a month, when you add up all the little spendings, you will find that you have a huge amount. Avoid daily trips to the grocery store for items that you have forgotten. These daily trips have the potential to damage your budget.

Deal with this by setting aside a day or even three days for no spending. If you don't have the correct ingredients, why not improvise?

Rock your budget

Challenges of budgeting and how to get around them

Now that you know how to create a budget, you have learned how you can stick to a budget; you have even written down everything and made appropriate plans for your next financial month. But one thing that you haven't learned are the challenges that you need to expect as you start your journey to living according to the budget you have created.

Let's face it—sticking to a budget is like riding a roller coaster. Therefore, you need to be ready to handle the bad side. If not, you may realize that you are off the rails. In other words, you'll have fallen off the budget wagon, and it is not easy to get back on.

So, get ready to learn some of the most significant budgeting problems that you will face. It is crucial that you know how to troubleshoot these problems because that is the only way you can be sure to remain on the budget wagon.

Understanding your finances can be difficult. You could be a conservative while your partner is a spender. Or even unexpected events happen in life, and you don't have a plan B to remove you from the unplanned situation. Whatever it is, you are going to learn different ways that you can plan ahead so that in case of an emergency, or when one of these most significant problems happen, you can remain strong and overcome them.

First, you need to know the most common budgeting problems that everyone seems to experience; then you can learn how you can overcome them. You will be ready before something emerges out of the blue, and you need to struggle to come up with a solution. You will also discover how to deal with unavoidable expenditures so that you don't break the bank.

When it comes to matters related to the budget, one of the most significant problems that people face is maintaining motivation. It is easy to come up with reasons to overspend. There will always be events to attend, tempting restaurant meals, and many more. In other words, you will have a lot of opportunities to tempt you.

Since life is too short to avoid having fun and spending time with family, you don't need to eliminate all the fun or swear that you will never dine out. Not only will you be unrealistic, but it's a sure way to prepare yourself to fail. The fun fact is that we all need to enjoy ourselves. And so, the secret is to plan and list down the fun things in the budget so that when they arise, you can dive in to experience the fun.

While reading the following section, you are advised to take out your budget and watch out for the most significant budgeting problems, so that you can be equipped on how to fix them, and continue to stay on track.

1. Get everyone on board

For married couples, it takes time to understand and learn each other. Maybe you like something, but your partner doesn't like it. The right thing is to talk about it. Tell him or her about your goals for your mutual future and the future of your kids. If you can see it together, you can then begin to implement the steps to attain your financial goals.

Are you stuck? If talking it out fails to work, and you are at your wit's end, give something to your spouse that they want. This can be an Xbox, a weekend away or even a concert ticket.

2. Feeling like you are losing all the fun

When you start to follow your budget, one of the biggest problems you will experience is that things will begin to look different. At one point, you will consider certain things as not fun enough.

But keep in mind that the fun is not over yet. You are still going to have your date night. You can still get out on weekends to play games with your friends. You will still have the time to party and interact with your family. You only need to plan and identify small ways to save while you enjoy yourself.

When you want to save on experiences, it is good to focus on the activity instead of the souvenirs. If you travel somewhere, focus on having a lovely experience, but set a budget in advance. Come only with the amount of money that you want to spend to take pictures, and have fun instead of trying to bring the fun home with you.

Take advantage of seasonal activities. During summer times, visit local sporting events, play games, and make use of free fun in your neighborhood. During winter, enjoy the flavors, sights, and sounds of the season. Look for means to enjoy the different light displays and other free but fun activities. You can throw yourself into the spirit of any season without spending any money.

3. Scared of making meaningful holiday memories

Christmas, birthdays, and even Easter are events that are populated with food, fun, and candy. Most people think of gifts and presents they are going to hand over to their loved ones. This, if not well budgeted, can damage your budget. So what can you offer for holidays and special events, and still ensure that the gift remains meaningful?

If you didn't know, the most meaningful gifts are not the most expensive. You can give out photo gifts because they aren't costly, but they are significant and touching for those who receive them.

Another awesome cheap gift that you can present is gift baskets. You can give out gift baskets containing homemade goodies, treats, and DIY items. You can even create "theme" baskets that have chapsticks, mini trashcans, tissues, and other go-to products that you require on the road. This can be a massive idea that your friends and loved ones will love.

4. Experiencing expensive emergencies

Your emergency fund should be a crucial aspect of your budget. Before you begin to pay your debt or save something, it is essential that your emergency fund is operational. Your emergency fund should be like your insurance policy. Regardless of what takes place, you will be covered because you have saved about $2,000 to cover any unexpected event.

Many people maintain a credit card "for emergencies". If you are one of those people, then you need to start to eliminate plans to have it as your emergency option. If you are serious about a budget and want to move forward to control your finances, then you must stop increasing your debt.

Consider this: emergencies take place. We just don't know when they will happen. A day is going to come up when you are going to require a lot of money. This means that if you have your emergency fund in place, you can deal with the situation fast because the money is already there.

But what happens when an emergency pops up, and you don't have your emergency fund? What will you do if you need money?

First, you must evaluate whether it is an emergency or not. Some situations, such as vacations, parties, and concerts, aren't emergencies. Typically, when you start to question whether it's an emergency or not, the chances are that it's not an emergency. Everyone knows when a situation is an emergency.

When it is an emergency, you need to remain calm. Request for a reduction in the payment plan or look for a means to work it into your budget. Try to reduce the damage as much as you can.

5. You are scared of cooking at home when you've got the option to go out

Eating out with friends is fun. Besides that, it is the easiest option. Someone else prepares the food and brings it to the table. You must eat and pay the bill. There is no stress at all. There's no struggling to wash dishes, forks, and spoons. But what if someone else told you that it's easy to prepare the same food in fifteen minutes? With some tips on easy meal planning, you can prepare food for your family without sweating. The good thing with this is that there are countless free online recipes and tips to plan your meals easily. In other words, you won't stay in the kitchen for long. In fact, you will spend less time compared to eating out trips.

6. Being worried about letting others down

Mothers and wives find it hard to say no. In fact, some feel guilty about it; they feel like they are letting down their loved ones when they refuse to go out with them and have some dinner or enjoy themselves.

Listen up. If there is something that you must know it is that your friends and family will never be happy seeing you in debt. They want to spend time with you. And the good news is that you don't need to spend much money to experience quality time with your friends. What about if you invite your friends and family over for a game night? Grill out in the summer? Or host a potluck? Tell them your plans and goals, and finally ask for their support. They will be happy to hear from you. The chances are that they could also be in the same lifeboat as yours, so they would love the idea of having cheaper fun.

For kids, there are many things that they may demand from you as a parent. However, most of these things aren't that costly. Most of the things that children will ask for are possessions that will make them happy, healthy, and well adjusted.

Rather than concentrate on buying physical items, you can consider spending time with your kid together as a family. Be playful with your kids. Ask them about their day and listen to what they want to tell you—you will be surprised that they are just fine.

How to overcome your top budgeting challenges

Budgets are the center of your financial solution. However, the significance of a budget doesn't make the process easy. When it comes to issues related to profit and expenses, it's a good thing to make as few mistakes as possible. Learning some of the challenges that emerge when you create your budget goes hand in hand with ensuring that your financial planning is comprehensive.

With some planning and foresight, you can make your finances work for you, rather than you working. Below are some tips that will help you overcome the biggest budget problems:

Getting that freedom

Some people think that budgets are restrictive because they will identify where, when, and how you are going to spend your money. However, this is the wrong perspective. One thing with a reasonable budget is that it will give you freedom. It will ensure that all the must-have expenses are taken care of, and you have money to spend on the things you want, not just those that you need. If you think your budget is depriving you of that freedom, take the time to review your spending for every month and remember that figure. That is the amount of money you can spend, and if you can afford to stay under it, you will be on the path to making more money.

Don't wait; get started

One of the main problems that people face after creating a budget is how to start. Don't wait for anything; the earlier you start, the better.

Set your goals

A budget must have financial goals tied to it. That is one of the reasons why you created it. The challenge in coming up with a goal is to understand the level of strictness you want to set. Some people believe that a goal is something you need to work extremely hard to achieve; others think a goal should be something reasonable that is easy to accomplish without working too hard. Ensure that you set multiple goals or even grades of success. If you set a high target, falling short of your target would be defined as missing the mark. Coming close would be considered excellent work.

Useful Money Lessons from the Richest Man in Babylon

If you are one of those people who think you are late to manage your money, think again:

1. First, pay for yourself – "Start thy purse to fattening."

This means that you must learn to see the value of your work and make it a purpose to pay yourself. Develop a simple system that can monitor the money you spend. This could be something like:

- 20%=Pay yourself.
- 10%=Pay your debts.
- 15%=Your future savings.
- 5%=Goes to church/non-profit organizations.
- 50%=Living costs.

2. Learn to live within your means – "Control thy expenditures."

Living within your means requires that you avoid spending more than you earn or make. You have two options: either spend less or increase your income. Again, you must learn to distinguish between a desire and an expense. Finally, avoid the tendency to spend more as you earn more. Just because your income will increase, doesn't imply you pay more.

3. Secure your wealth – "Guard thy treasures against loss."

- Have different insurance policies and means of income protection.
- Build an emergency fund.
- Avoid getting into investments that are too good to be true.
- When stuck, ask a friend or expert in that field for some advice.
- Make friends with people who have experience in what you are seeking.

4. Create a retirement plan – "Ensure a future income."

It is true that a time will come when you will not have the same energy as now to make money the way you do. You will grow old and become weak. It is important to start to plan for this day as early as possible before you retire. Look for alternative options to optimize your earnings. The thing is to have a plan in place where your income will continue to work without you being there. Diversify your investments to increase your safety.

5. Let money work for you – "Make thy Gold Multiply."

Learn about the power of compound interest and how it can be your good friend:

- Bank interest. Look for a high online interest account that you cannot access with your ATM card.
- Investments. Only opt for investments after you have saved a reserve of six-eight months' worth of your living expenses.
- There are many investment tools that you can select.

6. Have your own home – "Make of thy dwelling a profitable investment."

If you can, own your home. Become smart about your largest expense—if it's not home ownership. Purchase a home that is below the maximum you can manage, but one which you can enjoy.

7. Invest in improving yourself – "Increase thy ability."

Aim to become wise and knowledgeable. It is important to understand that the world we live in now is exciting. This is the era of information where things keep changing. So you need to be knowledgeable. One approach that you can employ to run your business involves Learning=>Earning=>Get=>Give.

More tips

- Your ability to manage money successfully will determine whether you can realize your dreams and desires.
- It costs nothing to seek some wise counsel from a good friend. For that reason, when you are stuck, ask for help.
- Saving money is crucial, but so is the feeling of fulfillment. Learn to enjoy life without feeling depressed.
- Paying your debt is great to show that you respect yourself.
- Remember: "The soul of a free man looks at the world as a series of problems to be solved. Meanwhile, the soul of a slave whines, 'What can I do?'"

Chapter 4: Simple Ways to Save Every Day

Nowadays, with the increased instant gratification, it is vital to remain focused on the goal of saving money in any possible way. To help you track your spending habits and reduce the expenses, here are simple ways to save money every day. Let's get right to the means to save money.

How to save money on groceries

- **Meal plan**

Meal planning is useful to your budget and a healthy body. Develop a calendar of meals for each week, starting with your kitchen. Find out what you already have, and identify what's on sale at the store and check recipes. Dinner should not be the only thing that you have to plan out. You also need to plan for lunch, breakfast, snack foods, and beverages. If you create your grocery list and prepare meals based on what's on sale in a particular week, you will save more money and waste less.

- **Don't buy what is not on the list**

It is time to be serious with yourself. Are you ready for that? Say the following words in your head: *It's not on my list.* The sales in the store should guide a well-written grocery list. This list is essential because it helps a person from forgetting.

- **Never shop hungry**

You may have heard this before. If you go shopping while hungry, you will be guided by your hunger, or overspend.

- **Create a shopping list**

Once you know your meals per week, and the type of ingredients you need, you can build a list of everything you need. The most attractive shopping lists are arranged by aisle. This ensures that you continue going to shop. It is one of the most natural means to be caught up in a flashy temptation.

- **Have a simple supper**

"Meat and three" is one of the most common meal misconceptions. You can have a great dinner without splurging on the price of ingredients. Apart from it being cheaper to change, it is also simple. Don't be scared of having a simple supper. This can be fantastic as a full dinner, but it can also be included in other meals with some critical planning.

- **Sample food, but don't buy**

You could accept to sample a portion of food if you were asked, "Would you like a sample?" But don't forget your primary focus. You have a list to follow and a goal of saving to fulfill. Don't feel obliged to buy food simply because you tested it.

- **Take advantage of store incentives**

Reward points, fuel cards, and shopper's cards. Identify the type of store that has the best offer then take advantage of it.

- **Try out grocery stores**

Loyalty is an important quality in employees and friends, but don't allow blind loyalty to make you go back to the grocery store that doesn't rhyme well with your budget. It is said, "You better shop around." Search for online store promotions. Let friends tell you where they go and why. Those who prefer the music selection over the loudspeaker aren't the best to listen to. Those who say they started to save hundreds before they shifted to the grocery store are the ones to listen to. With all the information, get into a new environment and test in reality.

- **Order groceries online**

Have you ever considered ordering your groceries online? Now, you can complete your virtual shopping cart from any place. Check the options you want: pickup or delivery. Consider the extra expenses. Some stores don't charge the following service, while some do charge. But don't be discouraged by the fee. If you are sidetracked in the actual store, this option will force you to shop by following a plan. You will probably save a lot in the long run or even no fee. In addition, you will complete a virtual cart, and you can easily monitor your spending. You can delete certain items or even look for cheaper options before you checkout, and you cannot be surprised by the total in the end.

- **Use a service**

Try out an internet meal-planning service such as eMeals. Every week, they will send a new recipe, along with a full shopping list arranged by the grocery organization. This prevents you from unnecessarily buying while you shop and from going to eat out because of the thrill of eating at home.

- **Coupon**

Whether you clip or select an item, don't forget its potential. Most supermarkets feature mobile apps with many coupons that will score more savings. Download the apps as you take advantage of the grocery list. However, don't buy something just because you have a coupon. If you are not going to eat it, you don't need it.

- **Be generic**

Not in who you are but in the choice of your brand. In most cases, off-brand and name-brand products will have a slight difference in ingredients and quality. It is okay to choose your best cereal or coffee as long as you budget for it.

- **Look at the price per ounce**

Which is a good deal: the 5 ounces of sour gummy that goes for $2.95 or the 10 ounces that sells for $7.95? Most stores do the above division for you, and it's right in the tag. When you doubt anything, your phone has a calculator. The price that is divided by ounce is equivalent to the price per ounce. A more significant choice is always cheaper.

- **Purchase in bulk**

Buying things in bulk is one of the best ways to save. Before you buy anything in bulk, ask yourself the following questions:

- Can I eat it before it goes bad?
- Is the price per ounce cheaper?
- Do I have space for the largest quantity?
- Can I use it?

Depending on the way you respond, you will know whether you need to purchase in bulk or not.

- **Avoid using credit cards**

One of the reasons why you are discouraged from using credit cards is that they create the mindset of spending money. Even if you always pay off your balance at the end of each month, it is straightforward to overspend when the money does not come out of your bank account.

- **Beware of the bakery**

The sweet aroma of freshly baked cakes, bread, and cookies is a great temptation to everyone. It calls you from the time you step through the automatic sliding doors. If it is not on your list, don't let this aroma tempt you into unnecessary buying.

- **Keep non-food products away from your grocery budget line**

It is important to separate your transactions if you select your household or beauty products together with your groceries.

- **Be real towards the end of the month**

Perform a reality check of yourself as you close out your budget at the end of the month. Compare what you have budgeted versus what you usually spend. Are your expectations reasonable or unreasonable? If you think that certain things aren't in line, you can adjust a bit.

How to save money at restaurants

- **Go early**

It is said that the early bird catches the worm, and so the early eater will get a nice deal. Most restaurants offer a nice discount to people who are ready to eat outside the usual dining hours. You may still eat at your favorite places and pay much less.

- **Sign up for emails**

The last thing that you want to see in your inbox is a promo email subscription, but the deals that you receive can be quite good. Exclusive digital coupons, offers, regular reminders of specials, and digital coupons will emerge without any effort on your side for the initial sign up. You can decide to unsubscribe later in case the emails don't provide enough, or when your cravings for a coconut-cream-pie-flavored doughnut end.

- **Purchase used or discounted gift cards**

You can buy online gift cards using sites such as Raise and Cardpool. Review your warehouse store for deals on the gift cards to your preferred restaurant.

- **Avoid appetizers**

If the choice of your restaurant provides complimentary bread or chips, then you can forgo purchasing the appetizer. Save about $8 by nibbling on the free stuff before your main comes.

- **Drink water**

If you are keen to look at the restaurant menu, you will see that they sell a bottle of drinking water. A quick way to save yourself some dollars is by ordering a glass of water.

- **Go to places where you serve yourself**

If you enjoy eating out, you can still save yourself 18% by going to places where you will serve yourself. You know the place where you order before you sit. One thing you are sure about places without servers is that you won't have to tip anyone. Serving jobs pay peanuts, and the people who work as servers depend on your tip. However, remember that saving money by skipping the tip isn't a great idea.

- **Go on a Monday or Tuesday**

Most restaurants don't have good traffic on Mondays and Tuesday because people are trying to eliminate the weekend moods. This means there are plenty of promotions on Monday and Tuesdays.

- **Avoid popular holidays**

Fixed-price menus have become very common for popular holidays. For only $49 per person, you can be served with a three-course meal, but what if you want $15? This is the reason why you need to avoid eating out on favorite holidays.

- **Save the lunch money**

Preparing your lunch at home is one of the best ways to save yourself some serious cash. If you are going to eat out five days per week for your mid-meal and spend $25-$60 per week, this means you will be spending $200 per month, which you can save by starting to prepare your meals at home.

How you can save money on everyday products

- **Sell or use your gift card**

If you have lots of unused gift cards, you can turn them into cash by swapping with friends.

- **Say no to credit cards**

One of the quickest methods to save money is to spend only what you have. Avoid using credit cards and don't be tempted to use a store credit card—they simply convince you into buying current "wants"; little do you know that you are entering into a long cycle of debt.

- **Place a shopping list on your fridge**

When you realize that you need additional toothpaste, toilet paper, etc., write down a small note on the ongoing shopping list. Don't wait until the last minute. Quick and short trips for these things mean that you are going to spend more. Keep in mind that these small extra outings add up to your whole budget. That is why the best thing is to keep a close eye on the items and make a small note when the supplies run low.

- **Use public transport or walk**

Well, it could be convenient to drive, but did you know that driving is not cost-effective? According to Andrei Vasilescu, the CEO of the money-saving site "DontPayFull", you should avoid driving your car to work.

He instead recommends that you use public transport such as buses, trains, or even shared vehicles. This will help your wallet because public transport is cheap. Keep in mind that owning a car has many additional costs, such as parking fees, insurance, and many more.

- **Look for financial planning apps**

Financial planning goals could be the best effortless means to save money every day because they are integrated with your account to monitor your spending and send you alerts when a problem arises.

Apps such as Wally, Mint, and Acorns build a budget and alert you when you are spending too much.

- **Organize a potluck**

Having more friends means the more cash you will spend on lunch dates, gifts, and birthdays. Instead of coming together for a nice dinner, arrange a potluck and let everyone bring his or her favorite dish. This way, you can spend the money on restaurant extras like tips and parking.

- **Look for lodging rental websites**

Finding a good place to spend a night while traveling is awesome, especially when you use rental websites such as House trip, Airbnb, or even Travelmob. You can always look for a place that has a kitchen so that you can prepare some food and save money.

- **Prepare your coffee at home**

Most people enjoy takeaway coffees. However, spending $4-$5 on a coffee every day soon adds up.

- **Wait 48 hours before clicking on "buy"**

Since it is possible to get anything that we want with just a simple click of a button, you need to come up with a system to help you handle your impulse buying.

For example, give yourself 48 hours before you spend money on products that cost more than what you should allow for. When you do that, you will realize that the item you wanted to buy was just a "want" and not a "need". In addition, you will save your money and work toward being aware of your spending.

- **Outsource online**

Time is a crucial resource, and your time is valuable. Nowadays, there are many tasks that you can outsource and thus save yourself a great deal of time and money. How can you determine whether you need to outsource something?

A great way to go about this is by calculating the time which will help you to determine whether you should pay someone to do something for less than your hourly rate.

- **Go for quality rather than quantity**

This one applies to clothes, food, and electronics. While it is tempting to go with the budget-friendly type, sometimes, selecting a quality product instead of quantity will save you some dollars.

- **Look online for promo codes**

Google, Coupons.com, and retailmenot.com should be your friends. Before you buy anything, look for discounts. Free shipping, percentages off, and specific-item discounts will emerge before your very eyes.

- **Sign up for balance alerts**

If your bank can allow you to set your notification to alert you when the account is going low, then do it.

- **Discuss with your internet provider**

Many internet providers offer an introductory rate and then begin to increase the rate by $30-$40 when you want to renew it. Call them and find out whether they can do better until a person is ready to listen and reduce the rate.

- **Downsize your house**

There are many reasons why you will want to downsize. It could be because of the mortgage.

- **Control your emotions**

Too much spending is a means to avoid experiencing certain emotions. If you run a personal check of yourself before you "spoil" yourself, you may identify areas that are making you feel bored, stressed, and lonely. As a result, you are spending money to fulfill your emotion. Review yourself before you purchase, and be mindful of your spending.

- **Read a personal finance book**

By reading books about personal finance, you will learn useful methods that can help you save money for a lifetime. Also, knowledge is the secret to becoming wealthy and successful.

- **Breakdown your financial goals**

You need to get specific with your financial goals. For instance, if you say, "I want to save for a home down payment," this is still not enough. It is vital that you specify the amount you need, by when, and what you need to do to save each month for attaining the goal. By knowing your target, you are likely to remain focused and continue to save until you hit the target.

- **Barter for repairs**

When you want to hire an expert to offer you help in a specific area, you can consider doing a barter program. For example, they fix the light in the kitchen, and you tutor their child.

- **Recheck your bills**

There is a high chance that you could save a vast sum of money on your fixed monthly bills. These are simple things that you can ignore because you have paid the same amount each month for what appears like forever. But are you missing out on special rates for your cell phone? What about your monthly gym membership?

- **Switch your insurance agents**

Many people set the renter's insurance and leave it like that. However, things change over time. Recheck your insurance. You can look for an independent insurance agent whom you can speak to. The loyalty is upon you and not a specific company.

- **Change your energy appliances and install energy-efficient devices**

While you replace your appliances, consider upgrading them to better energy-savers. These will save energy, and in turn, save you money. If it appears to be a huge investment now, begin small. You can start by replacing your light bulbs with the ones that have the Energy Star logo, and you will realize that you can save around $75 per year.

- **Monitor your progress**

Americans save about 5.5% of their money as compared to 20% that personal finance recommends. Instead of feeling embarrassed by your lack of savings, you should start by saving small.

How you can build more wealth

Thomas J. Stanley, the author of *The Millionaire Next Door*, describes three ways that you can build more wealth:

- The first step to creating wealth is to save part of your income.
- Anyone can build wealth no matter the state of their financial education or condition.
- You can build your wealth if you choose to concentrate on being resourceful, generate multiple streams of income, and focus on saving.

Even if you don't come from a wealthy background, you can still become wealthy.

No matter your financial condition, building wealth scales down to three aspects: saving, income optimization, and resourcefulness.

According to the co-author of the book, William D. Danko, true prosperity is the accumulation of good wealth and happiness.

In a Q&A with *The Washington Post*, Danko was requested to give his best advice for growing wealth:

"Regardless of your financial situation and education, first, commit to saving 20% of your income. Currently, most save about 5%. It is hard to get ahead as an investor without saving first."

Secondly, you need to learn to become a good steward of your resources. This should include having a stable personal relationship and positive personal habits. The above behaviors will build a long life and multiple opportunities.

Third, have a different stream of income. A second job can be significant.

Dedication to saving your income is an important aspect of defining your financial goals. Additionally, it is the secret to growing any wealth. In particular, 20% should be kept for an emergency fund, paying the debt, and retirement.

Even if you cannot save that amount now, that is the amount that you need to focus on.

In other words, spending all your income means that you cannot grow your financial net wealth. You have to train self-imposed financial scarcity. This means, if you make $100,000, you can build a lifestyle that demands 80% of this money and saves the rest.

The longer you stay, the longer the savings and investments will accrue compound interest. That is why you are advised to begin investing as early as possible.

According to research, a healthy personal life will result in a longer life. In fact, studies indicate that building a friendship is the secret to aging well and increasing your happiness. In addition, some personal habits, like changing your diet and doing the right body exercise, are important.

Lastly, when you generate more income, you will be able to earn more money and save—as long as you don't become one of the victims of "lifestyle creep". This will assist you in creating more passive income.

Ways to spend money wisely

Frugal living doesn't mean you deprive yourself of all the fun. In fact, you may be surprised to learn how easy it can be to scale your expenses as long as you are patient and plan well. The more you can save from every bit of money you spend, the higher the amount of money you will have. Below are seven ways to spend money wisely:

1. Aim for quality where it is important

The cheapest option is the most expensive one. There is no need to buy something for $30 and then after three months buy another one. It is better to spend $60 on a product that will last you for the next year. This way, you know that you will save both money and time.

2. Clip on coupons for specific offers

Eating out is a fun activity, but if you are not disciplined, it can empty your wallet faster than you realize. Restaurants are generally generous with the kinds of deals they give, so you should begin to clip for some serious cash.

3. Wait for it

As a shopper, you must learn the art of being patient. Patience is the game that will win you great rewards.

4. Go for generic label groceries

Most people like to buy brand products instead of going for generic labels. Though these people believe that they are buying a quality product, the truth is that brand products are priced high because of the marketing expenditure. In other words, the product is sold higher because they want to compensate for their marketing budget.

5. Don't purchase specialized products

When buying products, go for products that have different uses instead of single specific use. For instance, do you need to buy a special tool to assist you in peeling an orange when a knife can do the same work? Do you need an ice cream scooper when a regular spoon can do the same work? Do you require a separate printer, scanner, or fax machine when you can get everything in a single device?

6. Don't go shopping with people who like to shop

If you don't want to overspend on shopping, you better make sure that you don't walk into the grocery store with your friend who is addicted to shopping. The reason is that you will be infected with the same habit, and by the time you reach home, your wallet will already be empty. Keep in mind that some friends are only good for hanging out, but not when you want to go shopping.

Other ways to save money every day

- Turn off the television
- Stop collecting and begin to sell
- Register for free customer rewards
- Create your gifts rather than buy from the store
- Master the 30-day rule. This rule teaches you to deal with instant gratification, and wait 30 days before you buy anything
- Repair clothing rather than toss it

- Don't spend a lot of money entertaining your kids
- Try to negotiate a rate with your credit card company
- Clean out your closets
- Purchase video games that have the most replay value and don't look for new ones until the time you master what you have
- Drink enough water
- Say no to convenience foods and fast foods
- If you are a smoker, enroll in a program to quit smoking
- Turn off the lights when you aren't using a room
- Swap books, DVDs/Blue-rays, and music at the library or the internet.
- Optimize yard sales
- Install LEDs or CFLs wherever it is reasonable
- Install a programmable thermostat
- Change or clean your car's air filter
- Compare prices, and go for the cheaper grocery store
- Avoid impulse spending
- Do maintenance check on your appliances
- Buy used products if possible
- Remove your credit card numbers from your online accounts
- Do your holiday shopping immediately after the holidays
- Stick to reliable fuel efficient cars
- Avoid going to the mall
- Rent unused space in your home

- Build a visual reminder of your debt
- Unsubscribe from magazine subscriptions
- Don't be scared of leftovers
- Brown bag your lunch
- Go through all your clothes
- Train yourself to dress minimally
- Try to fix things yourself
- Invest in a deep freezer

Lessons in building wealth from *The Millionaire Next Door*

If you want to become a millionaire, you will probably have to begin by learning the actions of millionaires. Look for popular financial books, and you are bound to find different books, including *The Millionaire Next Door*.

The main concept of the book is that "people who look rich may not be rich" probably spend more using tools of wealth. These people may have great portfolios and some large debts. Conversely, actual millionaires may be living in "middle-income neighborhoods" and drive economical cars.

You may have come across the book, or even be acquainted with the concept. Maybe you read it a long time ago. If you reread it, you will start to remember the great wisdom Stanley and Danko discovered from their many years of analyzing millionaires.

Without further ado, here is a lesson from the book:

Lesson 1: Income doesn't equal wealth

Of course, high-income homes tend to have more wealth than other homes. However, the amount of income only reveals a 30% difference in wealth among homes. So what is important is how much of your income you invest. On average, millionaires are said to save around 20% of their earnings.

Danko and Stanley provide a formula to determine whether your net worth corresponds with your income:

> Multiply your age times your realized pretax annual household income from all sources except inheritances. Divide by 10. This, less any inherited wealth, is what your net worth should be.

Lesson 2: Know where your dough doth go

"Do you know how much your family spends every year on food, shelter, and clothing?" Approximately "two-thirds of millionaires," say "yes" to this question. On the other hand, only "35% of high-income millionaires" say yes to the above question.

Lesson 3: Know where you want your money to go

Two-thirds of millionaires responded affirmatively to the following question: "Do you have a well-defined set of weekly, daily, monthly, and yearly goals?"

Lesson 4: Work that budget

Many millionaires operate on a budget. Those without a budget, they are said to have what is referred by Stanley as "an artificial economic environment of scarcity,"—more commonly referred to as "pay yourself first." In other words, they invest a big chunk of their money before beginning to spend.

Like the authors say, "It's much easier to budget if you visualize the long-term benefits of this task."

Lesson 5: Time is money

All plans of creating a budget and setting goals consume time, but millionaires are ready to commit. Prodigious wealth accumulators spend most hours planning for their investments as "under accumulators of wealth." Most prodigious accumulators acknowledged the following statements, while most of the under accumulators did not.

- "I spend a lot of time planning my financial future."

- "Usually, I have enough time to manage my investments properly."
- "When it comes to the allocation of time, I place the management of my assets before any other activity."

You don't need to be earning big to plan. In a survey conducted by Stanley and Danko on 854 middle–income workers, they discovered a "strong positive correlation" between investment planning and accumulation of wealth. This additional planning doesn't just work. According to Danko and Stanley, "Most PAWs have a regimented planning schedule. Each week, each month, each year, they plan their investments."

Lesson 6: Love the spouse you are with

Many wealthy guys only marry one person and remain committed to this person for the rest of their years.

Of course, marriage should not be defined by money. However, different studies have proven that married people make more wealth than single or divorced people.

But it's important when choosing a person to marry that you marry a person with the right financial habits. According to Danko and Stanley, in most of the millionaire homes, the husband was the breadwinner and seemed to be frugal, but the wife is even more. As they put it, "A couple cannot accumulate wealth if one of its members is a hyper-consumer."

Lesson 7: Love the home you are in

The choice of your home will determine your potential to make wealth. Stanley and Danko found that half of the millionaires tended to live in a house for over twenty years.

In *Stop Acting Rich,* also written by Thomas Stanley, he dives deeper into how your house affects your spending. He says, "Nothing has a greater impact on your wealth and your consumption than your choices of house and neighborhood."

He further says, "[People] who live in million-dollar homes are not millionaires. They may be high-income producers but, by trying to emulate glittering rich millionaires, they are living a treadmill existence."

If you are planning to purchase a home, Stanley offers you this simple advice, "The market value of the home you purchase should be less than three times your household's total annual realized income."

Lesson 8: Don't drive away your wealth

Most wealthy people own their cars instead of leasing. About a quarter drive the latest model, and the other quarter drive cars older than four years. More than a third of millionaires like to purchase used vehicles. According to *Stop Acting Rich*, Toyota is the most common type of vehicle used by millionaires.

Now, a question that you could be asking is: who is driving a Mercedes and BMW then? Not millionaires. For your information, 86% of prestige cars are purchased by non-millionaires. Stanley even writes that "one in three people who traded in their old car for a new one was upside down and owed more on the trade-in than its market value." It's quite difficult to become a millionaire doing such things.

Lesson 9: The rich are different; they are happier with their life

You could be wondering whether this idea of living below your means pays in the long run. Well, the millionaire has an extensive portfolio, but are they happy? According to *The Millionaire Next Door*, they are indeed satisfied.

Chapter 5: Investing for Beginners

If you want to become the next millionaire, you need to start investing your money. It only doesn't make sense if you don't invest. Even if you decide to invest 5% of your money, it's still going to create a difference in the future.

You need to know that investing is a smart move and that several people have made good money from investing. Maybe you want to invest, but you don't know how to start, or you could be scared to lose all your money, and you don't want to go back to square one to build your income.

The good news is that this chapter will introduce you to critical concepts about investing that you need to know.

You can master investing, and if you read all of this chapter, you'll learn the basics to get started. You don't need to be worried about losing all your money when you focus on the long term and follow the principles of an average investor.

You also don't need to do all the tasks nor offer all your returns to a delegated someone. You'll be depending on automation and allowing the computer to do the work for you.

After you complete this chapter, the only thing left for you to do will be to dive into action. Don't worry; you will be guided through the process. Whether you want to prepare for your retirement plan or save for your child's college, you will attain your goal faster by investing.

That said, **what is investing, and why should you care about it?**

In simple terms, investing can be defined as trading your money today with an expectation to make more in the future.

Putting your money into a business you build, or a home you live in is also a form of investment. There is also the stock market investment that is very popular. Investments are the high return you make in the long term—the key word here being "long term".

Some people are scared of the market. One common characteristic of people who fear the market is that they place much emphasis on their money.

As you know, banks don't like to give away their money. This mindset is shown in the interest rates that banks offer when it comes to checking and savings accounts.

When you deposit your money into the bank, the bank will invest in that cash at 7% per year or more. Once they make their profit, they will give a tiny percentage of it back.

Keep in mind that this is your money they are investing, so you deserve a bigger share. The only way to deal with the issue of a bank taking advantage of your money is to invest the money yourself.

That brings us to the next question:

Why invest?

Saving money isn't enough to build a wealth empire. While a bank will keep your money safe, every year, inflation will make each dollar you have saved less valuable. In other words, the dollar you keep in the bank today is going to be worth a little less in the following year.

On the other hand, when you choose to invest, your dollars will work to earn you more dollars. The new dollars will work to earn you even more dollars. Which again work to earn you more. This is called compound growth.

In the long term, investing will generate an opportunity for your assets to grow over and surpass the rate of inflation. Your initial savings grow instead of declining in value. This makes it significantly fast to save for long-term goals, such as retirement.

You will be crazy not to invest, and you will be equally crazy when you play around with your money on a checking and savings account because the difference is always small. If you didn't know, you're better off having 90% of your money sitting in a checking account, and 10% sitting in a checking account rather than 90% in a savings account.

Portfolio and diversification

Whenever you read a beginners guide to investing, you're likely to come across the terms "Portfolio" and "Diversification".

So what do these terms mean and why should you bother?

Everything you have is part of your portfolio. Your investment accounts, retirement accounts, and even your home are forms of investments. Your portfolio doesn't include a savings and checking account. The reason is simple: these are short-term assets. When it comes to the portfolio, it has to contain your long-term wealth building investment methods, but not the short term.

When should you invest?

If you haven't started investing yet, today is a great time to begin.

In general, you will want to start investing as early as possible so that you establish a solid financial foundation. This comprises of having no high-interest debt, a goal for your investment in mind, and an emergency fund. Doing so, it will allow you to leave the money invested for the long term.

Importance of starting young

When it comes to investing, the time you begin is critical. The longer time your money is invested, the longer it will have to work to build more money and take advantage of compound growth. It is also far less likely that one harsh market will highly affect your wealth as you'll have the time to leave the money invested and get back its value.

Pay off high-interest debt

If you know you have high-interest debt, then investing is an excellent way to pay your debt. Your money will work harder for you to remove that high-interest expense. Focus on coming out of debt as early as possible, then fully concentrate on investing.

Set aside an emergency fund

Time is a valuable tool when it comes to investing. To get started, you need to prepare yourself to allow the money to remain in the investment. If not, you reduce your time zone, and this could force yourself to pull money out at the wrong time.

To secure yourself from unexpected expenses, save enough emergency funds for your needs. Don't plan for your investment accounts to become a common source of cash.

Starting small is fine

Sometimes, people have this wrong idea that they cannot begin to invest until the time they have enough money. If this could be the case, many people would give up the years of compound growth waiting until the time they become rich. No matter how small your money is, it is advised to get that money working for you as early as possible.

The principles of investing

The world of investment is not a piece of cake. It can be complex. There are key investing principles that apply to everyone, whether you are a seasoned portfolio manager or a novice investor. It never hurts to spend some time analyzing the critical principles and enhancing the foundations based on which we make investment decisions.

Below are ten investment principles that are critical to success:

1. Adopt an investing strategy

It is crucial to be aware of the type of investor you are and stick to the principles of your investing strategy. If you decide to become a value investor, you are in the right place to learn. Your investment decisions have to be valuation-based. No matter your investing strategy, make sure you adopt a consistent strategy. This means, as a value investor, you should not involve yourself in momentum investing.

2. Invest with a specific interval of safety

If you purchase an asset for lower than its actual value, you will have a margin of safety. One of the most exciting things that you should remember is that price matters. The right plan to reduce risk is to purchase investments at a price that is lower than the intrinsic value.

A low price means a high value of appreciation if the situation is favorable. Similarly, a low cost will create a margin of safety if the circumstances are okay.

3. Asset allocation is the number 1

How you assign your portfolio among different asset categories is the biggest decider of your investment returns. If you place money into overvalued asset categories, you will get poor long-term returns. It is important that you overweight asset categories that are bargain-priced and avoid expensive asset categories.

4. Invest for the long term

Short-term investing is a drawback of current investing strategies. Great investors know that if you purchase an investment at an affordable price, it may take time for the market to understand its true value.

A long-term investment is one of the most crucial investing principles because of short-term trading results in long-term performance. This is popular because many investors allow fear and greed to cause them to make wrong decisions. The long term will deal with itself if you make a wise decision.

5. Maintain your expenses low

Many investors don't understand the difference which a high cost causes to their portfolio.

For instance, in 30 years, a rise in the expense of 1% will cost your portfolio more than the original principal.

6. Diversification is important

Investment diversification in small figures offers vast benefits. If you have five investments, you will earn more than two investments.

7. Use compounding to your advantage

Exponential growth is a great financial concept. Learn how it works for you and the reason why dividend growth compounding multiplies the value of compounding.

It is crucial to learn the devastation of reverse compounding. The more portfolios you lose, the harder it is to compensate because you lose principal. A 10% loss only deserves an 11% gain to return to break-even. But a 50% loss needs a 100% gain to return to break-even.

8. Control your destiny

Nobody cares more about your money than you do.

Technology and the internet have reduced transaction costs and offered ways to acquire information and guidance at a very lower cost.

Is investing right for me?

It doesn't matter whether you have planned to purchase your first share or selected a market to invest funds for the first time, always try to answer why you want to invest.

In the long run, historical stocks and share outrun money savings accounts.

Why don't you need a financial investor?

Everyone wants to be successful after a handful of investment years. The truth is that this doesn't always happen and is unlikely to occur.

That is important because we are aware that with enough patience and time, it is possible to find success. The problem happens when people run out of patience. They begin to look for shortcuts. One of the most common alternatives is recruiting a financial advisor.

There are many reasons why you shouldn't hire a financial advisor. Some include:

1. No one will work hard to help you build your wealth.

2. The option to avoid fees.

3. You may not get the best financial advisor

Where should you focus first?

When getting started in investing, it can be quite challenging to choose between numerous types of investment accounts. As you start, keep in mind to concentrate where you see the highest value.

Principles of smart investing

Successful investing requires a person to make the right choice that fulfills special needs and financial goals of the future:

1. Understand yourself

Everyone has different goals of investing and different time frames to achieve the said goals. Some are short term, others long term.

Although risks may look like things that you can avoid, greater risk can provide the chance for greater rewards in the long term.

To understand yourself as the investor, you need to focus on your investment knowledge, gross annual income, estimated net worth, gross yearly income, and investment time interval.

2. **Find an early start**

Take advantage of the power of compounding; this is one of the methods to make your money work for you.

3. **Make regular investments**

It is easier to develop a smaller amount to invest weekly or monthly than make a huge ton of money. A consistent investment strategy will allow you to pick when and how you want to make contributions.

Tips for smart investing

Building wealth requires total commitment to ensuring that the money works for you. Below are some of the cautions to consider while investing:

Be realistic

Investing doesn't involve looking for the highest profit. Focus on your investment objectives to make realistic investment decisions that will allow you to achieve your financial goals. Set the investment objectives by applying the SMART model to set your goals.

Follow a comprehensive plan

Come up with a plan to reduce the urge to purchase or sell investments without careful thought. List the plan down and set the dates to analyze it periodically. Building your plan will assist you both in good and bad times, and it will allow you to evaluate the wild tips you receive from your family member/s.

Avoid trouble

Make sure you conduct thorough research before you begin to invest to help you remain comfortable with your decisions.

Don't trust others blindly

Remember that this is your money. Think for yourself and research any advice you hear before taking action.

Avoid fairy tales

If something looks too good to be true, perhaps it is. Put out red flags when a company or someone promises a significant profit on an investment.

Don't depend so much on past performance

Keep this advice: past performance is an achievement but doesn't guarantee the future.

Don't borrow to invest

If your investment doesn't come out well, then you will still have to pay the lender the money. That is the reason why you need to stick to your savings and investment goals that you set for investing.

Avoid getting emotional

When you have a plan, aim to stick to it to avoid committing mistakes and making impulsive decisions.

Basic Types of Investing

This is a refresher for investing. There is an endless list of investment types that you can make, but all investments fall in one or another category known as "asset classes". An asset class comprises of investments with the same features and is covered by the same set of financial rules.

Asset classes

The asset classes that many people know include:

1. Stocks

2. Fixed income investments

3. Cash

There are different asset classes you can explore when it comes to investing:

1. Commodities and futures, such as gold or oil

2. Alternative investments

3. Responsible, sustainable, and impactful investments with the main focus on useful social or important environmental effects.

Equity Investing

This involves the buying and selling of stocks using public companies. This is what comes to people's minds when they hear the term "investing" and is one of the most popular means of investing for starters.

Publicly traded companies provide investors with an equity interest through the buying of stocks.

By selling shares, companies can generate the capital to assist them in expanding.

Stock investors can purchase stocks from returns to increase the price of the stock. Stock investors can also acquire profit from the receiving stock dividends.

Stocks are traded on an exchange like the New York Stock Exchange. The exchange will facilitate the trading of stocks.

The most critical thing is to evaluate the stock price. One way is to assess the performance of the company. Another factor to consider is the general industry of which the company belongs, the performance of economic conditions, and government actions.

Stock investors are directed by their investment decisions mainly by technical analysis or fundamental analysis.

The Fixed Income Investing

Fixed income investing describes investments in debt securities that provide investors with a fixed rate interest payment over a given period. Debt securities are usually referred to as "bonds". The bond market is one of the largest markets across the world, thanks to the largest amount of debt that many governments have.

When you buy a bond, you will be offering to finance a government or company. In return, you get a specific size of interest called a "coupon rate". The interest bonds are always paid annually or semi-annually until you get the bonds for a full principal amount.

The coupon rate is the return offered on a bond at the time it is released. When the rate of interest continues to increase, the value of the bond, and its initial "yield to maturity" change. The coupon rates don't change in the course of a life of a bond, but the change in the interest rates will affect the value of the bond and yield.

For the investors who have bonds to maturity, the changing yield to maturity rates in the course of the life of the bond does not affect their investment yield.

Zero coupon bonds

Some bonds are released on "zero coupon bonds". Instead of providing regular interest payments, however, the zero coupon bonds are sold at a specific discount from the face value of the bond. Investors make a profit by buying the bond for lower face value and then go ahead to redeem the bond at maturity for the complete face value.

Bond Sellers-Corporations and Governments

The bonds are sold by the municipal governments and national governments. The municipal bonds are common because most bonds earn interest tax-free.

Besides that, government corporations offer bonds to get financing. Corporation bonds usually pay a higher rate of interest than similar government bonds. Corporate bonds are also very volatile compared to government bonds because its value is affected by the expected value of the corporate issuer.

Fixed investment income could attract investors that are planning for retirement and have an extensive amount of investment capital present during the many years of working. These investors can buy a vast size of bonds, gather interest payments while working, and then towards the time of their retirement, the bonds have grown and returned the face value to the investor.

Investing Do's and Don'ts

Usually, a bad mix of inexperienced investors and brokers can lead to a big financial crisis. Investors need to protect themselves by being educated and aware of the following tips:

- Don't get convinced by promises of "limited" or "no risk" returns.
- Do expand your knowledge about online investment fraud.
- Don't be deceived by high-yield investment schemes.
- Be aware of fraud linked to current events, such as oil or gas scams.
- Don't enter business with a broker or investment firm that you aren't familiar with.
- Do you know your investments?
- Don't start to invest without a plan or strategy.
- **Ask yourself a few questions before investing:**
    - Are the claims for investment true?
    - Does the investment fulfill your personal investment goal?
    - Are the seller and investment registered correctly?

- ♦ Has the seller provided you with written information to explain the investment?
- If the answer to any of the above questions is "no" you risk being defrauded.
- Don't invest before looking for other opportunities.
- Do act fast when you find a problem.
- Don't invest anything you don't know about.
- Don't invest in something just because others are investing in it or someone sold it to you.
- Don't pay a lot of money for investment products unless you understand the reason why the product is worth it.
- Don't make the assumption that someone advising you has their objectives aligned with yours.
- Don't become a victim to behavioral marketing tactics.
- Don't concentrate on the short term.
- Don't try to time the market.
- Do diversify your investments.
- Do extensive research.
- Don't wait.
- Do maintain cash savings.

Conclusion

Congratulations on reaching the end of this book. You should now have a solid understanding of the concept of debt. Realize that debt happens, and it is part of life. It can be as a result of a failed venture or a failed life. The good thing is that debt can be resolved as long as you are ready to become patient.

If you feel you have a better understanding of your finances and know how to create a budget that reflects your expenses, you have mastered the steps you need to do to pay off your debt. You have already started to save for your future, well done! You have succeeded in taking control of your finances and life.

However, some people will want to go that extra step and make their money work for them. This can be interesting and rewarding, but it can also be risky and complicated. Keep in mind the principles of investing. Remember the dos and don'ts we mentioned about investing. The last thing you want is to lose all the money that you spent years saving up. So, remember that not all types of investments will guarantee that you make money. Sometimes, you may lose the money that you already have.

Part 2: Credit Repair

The Ultimate Guide to Boosting Your Credit Score, Paying off Debt, Saving Money and Managing Your Personal Finances in a Stress-Free Way

Introduction

When you have a higher credit score, you have many advantages. For example, you can get credit cards with the best rewards, and the lowest rates on any loans.

If you want a mortgage, but you don't have the best credit score, you will have to pay a lot of interest.

A credit score is powerful because it can increase your probability of finding a job or even being accepted as a new tenant because landlords and employers look at your credit score. In other words, a credit score is the best financial estimate to reveal how responsible you are, and it goes to other areas of finance.

Once you are aware of what is on your credit report and how it impacts your score, you have no other choice but to look for ways to repair your credit. Fixing bad credit isn't something that can happen overnight, but again, you don't have to wait years before you see some positive changes.

You don't have to carry the burden of bad credit for your entire life. Begin making a change today by reading this book to learn how to repair your credit card, pay all your debts, save money, and manage all your finances.

Inside this book, you will learn the factors that affect your credit score and how you can fix them. We will also teach you why you need to pay all your debt and some of the ways you can apply to pay your debts. If you have been struggling to learn how to save money, or even how you can manage your finances, read on to discover methods that will allow you to start saving for your future.

Chapter 1: Boosting Your Credit Score

Your credit score has three numbers that lenders use to decide how likely they can be repaid on time if they provide you with a credit card or loan. This is a critical factor when it comes to your financial life. In other words, the higher your credit score is, the more likely you are to qualify for credit cards and loans at the most favorable terms, which saves you some money.

If you have a bad credit history, or it's in a state which you don't want it to be, you aren't alone. Improving your credit score takes time, but the earlier you begin to fix the issues that may be slowing it down, the faster your credit score will rise. It is possible to increase your credit score by taking a few steps, such as building a track record of paying your bills on time, paying down debt, and taking advantage of new tools that will let you add cell phone and utility bills to your credit file.

How to monitor and advance your credit score

When was the last time you looked at your credit? If it is longer than several months, you want to consider checking it. If it's longer than a year, then it's time to change the way you track your credit.

Keeping a close check on your credit enables you to understand the way your financial actions impact your credit. This will also help you to respond to any immediate change in your score and know when you have attained excellent credit, and you may qualify for better interest credit card offers. Alternatively, learning how your credit score changes over time gives you the ability to manage your financial wellbeing. However, it is vital to ensure that you monitor your credit score without damaging it.

Hard and soft inquiries and how they impact your credit

Credit requests, or inquiries about your credit report information, are categorized under soft and hard inquiries. A soft inquiry refers to any inquiry where a prospective lender isn't reviewing your credit. This can take place when you examine your credit score. Don't be scared; soft inquiries don't change your credit score, so don't be afraid to check it.

On the other hand, a hard credit request is when your credit is getting reviewed because you have applied for credit using a prospective lender. Hard inquiries consist of a sizable amount of your general credit score and tend to have the least, short-term effect. However, if you have many of them in the short term, it may indicate that you are a risky borrower. This may lead to a lower credit score.

Get to know your different credit scores

There are two major credit scoring models that lenders can apply to understand the risk:

- The FICO score
- VantageScore

Although each model has the same credit report, they analyze the information differently. Some consumers may check on a considerable difference between the two sources. The score that will be applied depends on the individual lender. However, the FICO Score is widely used. But the VantageScore is often used for free credit scores that you can get online.

Three main credit reporting bureaus or companies search for consumer data and develop credit reports. These credit reports are then used by companies to convert your credit history into a score. The three major bureaus include:

- Experian
- TransUnion
- Equifax

The credit report from each bureau will vary slightly because certain lenders can only report to one while others may report to all three bureaus. In other words, you will have three different FICO Scores, and the score applied will depend on which credit bureau the lender extracts your report from. Despite this, there shouldn't be huge differences among these scores.

Credit Score Monitoring services

There are different credit score monitoring services that you can access easily. You are eligible to a free credit report every year from main credit bureaus. This was an amendment that was done in 2003 in the Fair Credit Reporting Act. The free annual reports can be requested from AnnualCreditReport.com. Despite this, it is critical that you monitor your credit score more than once per year.

Continuous tracking of your credit score will give you the chance to realize any errors done and dispute them early. It will also provide you with a better understanding of the way your financial behavior impacts your credit score in real-time—this gives you the time to work on boosting your credit score. While your score increases, you will notice when it is high to qualify for a lower interest rate and better lending offers.

MyFICO.com provides a paid service that will allow you to track your credit score from different credit bureaus on a quarterly or monthly term. You can get reports from a single or all three bureaus and enjoy extra features, such as theft monitoring and 24/7 fraud resolution, based on the type of monthly subscription you select.

Experian will also provide a credit paid monitoring service for a monthly fee. They will send emails to your inbox every time there is a change in your credit score, along with an explanation so that you can understand your score better.

Credit cards that assist you in tracking your credit score

Your credit card may provide you with a free credit score tracking service. This feature is popular for credit cards designed to fix credit or bad credit cards. But several major credit card providers currently offer this service to all their customers.

Every credit monitoring program has its advantages. The list of issuers that have credit monitoring on most of their credit cards includes Chase, American Express, and Capital One.

If you want to avoid monthly fees, but still stay on top of tracking your credit, you can decide to use the free credit monitoring services from your credit card plus a detailed annual report from AnnualCreditReport.com. You can try the credit monitoring services from MyFICO.com and Experian as well, taking advantage of their free trial. Whichever option you decide to take, it is important that you stay in the loop when handling your credit score and the factors that affect it, and realize that doing so will not affect your credit score.

The three primary credit bureaus and how they operate

The popular credit bureaus have a significant effect on every consumer, but many people don't know these companies or how they work. The top three credit bureaus companies include:

- Experian
- Equifax
- TransUnion

These companies have a great history in the financial industry.

What is a credit bureau?

Also known as a credit reporting agency, it gathers financial information about consumers and combines this information into a single report. Since these bureaus work independently, the credit report that a single bureau generates for an individual could be slightly different from another bureau's report. Although there are smaller credit bureaus, the top three serve a more significant share of the market.

The credit bureaus have a fascinating profit model. Lenders, banks, and many other companies share a lot of information about their clients with credit bureaus for free. The credit bureaus process this information and put it on sale, in the form of a credit report, to different parties that require insight into your financial history, and more.

These credit reports are essential to financial institutions because they assist lenders in knowing individuals who would be profitable clients. If you don't have a credit report, your bank may not know the amount of money that is safe to lend or the interest rate to charge on a loan. For landlords, the credit report acts as an indicator to show whether you can manage to pay rent, and for employers, a good credit report is a symbol of reliability.

Credit reports

Your credit report has some but not all financial data from past and present. A credit report consists of a list of your current and past credit products, the amount of debt you are having, and any late payments or any payment issues that you may have experienced in the recent years. Serious problems such as bankruptcies and tax liens will also show up on the report. However, your credit report will not contain your job history, status of employment, income, and some personal information like your marital status.

Credit scores

Your credit score is determined from a complicated calculation by the credit bureau that summarizes everything from your credit report to show the amount of risk you can bring to lenders. A higher score indicates that you have an excellent payment record. This means that your debt load is low, and you act responsibly to lenders, which means you are a low-risk client. On the other hand, a low credit score implies that you tend to pay your debts late. If you don't have any credit history or it is quite low, then you will have a low score because the credit bureaus will have little information to decide whether you are a risk or not.

Not a single score but many

The challenge with credit scores is that there are different methods to compute them. Therefore, many people have different credit scores based on the type of credit bureau that provides the score. The two major credit scoring models include VantageScore and FICO, but any of these two scoring models come in different forms. Plus, certain items from your financial history may not be taken into account for all three credit bureaus, which can generate a big difference in the scores from those entities.

Making the best from credit bureaus

It is a little annoying to learn that all three credit bureaus have sensitive financial data. However, there's no method to prevent lenders and collection entities from sharing your information with the above companies.

You can limit any possible problems associated with the credit bureaus by evaluating your credit reports annually, and acting immediately in case you notice some errors. It is also good to monitor your credit cards and other open credit products to ensure that no one is misusing the accounts. If you have a card that you don't often use, sign up for alerts on that card so that you get notified if any transactions happen, and regularly review statements for your active cards. Next, if you notice any signs of fraud or theft, you can choose to place a credit freeze with the three credit bureaus and be diligent in tracking the activity of your credit card in the future.

Understanding and boosting your credit score

Whether you have a bad credit score, or you are working to have a credit score, this section is right for you because we shall guide you on how you can build your credit score to help you reach where you want, whether that is boosting your credit score from scratch, or repairing one that is broken.

Your credit health determines your financial future. In other words, when you have strong credit health, you get access to loans with a low-interest rate, and this will save you a lot of bucks in the long term. On the other hand, a bad credit score may limit your chances of getting funds to buy a vehicle, or get the best rates for a credit card.

The credit sector can be complicated, and even challenging to start. The first step to get a strong credit score begins with learning everything about your credit score. By mastering your credit score and the things to do to change it, you will crack your credit potential and realize your goals.

This section will teach you more insights about your credit score, and what you can do to improve it.

The definition of credit score

A credit score has three numbers that reveal much about your credit report, and lenders depend on this to define the health of your credit. An algorithm determines the scores of a credit. This algorithm relies on information from your credit report. Credit scores were developed to show the probabilities that you can achieve in your payment agreement.

There is a misconception that each is allocated a single credit score, which is accessed by lenders and bureaus. This is a lie because you can have multiple credit scores. And the reason is that there are many credit agencies, and different strategies to use to calculate information, and credit scores at different times. If you aren't aware, there are more than a hundred models of scoring, but the most popular models comprise of VantageScore and FICOScore.

Don't be scared about monitoring every credit score, but keep a close eye on the popular scores, which many lenders use to determine whether you qualify for a credit or not.

Learn more about your credit report

A credit report, as the name suggests, contains data and information that credit agencies get from lenders. In the United States, numerous credit agencies process a consumer's credit report. But the main credit agencies that most businesses and financial organizations use include TransUnion, Equifax, and Experian.

Credit reports are updated now and then depending on your credit activity and information you share with financial institutions and businesses. This consists of banks, mortgage firms, credit card firms, and lenders. Information on your credit report can be classified into three categories:

- Credit History
- Public records and collections
- Credit inquiries

Your credit report also has general information that describes more about you. For example, your social security number, name, date of birth and address. Some of the things that your credit report doesn't have include:

- Your occupation, salary, and date of employment (even if lenders want to know this information to approve your loan).
- Your daily spending habits.

Keep in mind that though lenders depend on information in your credit report to learn more about your credit history, there are other aspects not in your credit report that they use to make a decision.

According to the Fair Credit Reporting Act, you have the permission to ask for your credit report at the end of the year from each of the major credit reporting firms.

How is your credit score computed?

Credit bureaus have millions of data to process credit scores, but how do they access this data?

When it comes to matters to do with credit, financial firms such as credit card firms and banks have a dual duty. Many people focus on the role of approving credit. However, that is not the only responsibility they do; they also send out the information to credit bureaus concerning consumer's credit behavior, which is later added into credit reports.

Creditors and lenders who take part in any trade have to share the info about your credit history to the bureaus. This consists of information such as the amount paid, account balance, and the status of your account. A financial company requests each time you sign up for credit and a credit report from a credit bureau—it will be attached to your credit report in the form of a "hard inquiry".

Scoring institutions, such as VantageScore and FICO, require your credit information to determine your credit score. Both VantageScores and FICO extend between 300-850 and include five aspects into the scoring formula. Some of these factors include the age of accounts, credit utilization, types of credit in use, payment history, and new credit.

Top factors that affect your credit score

   1. **Your payment history**

The history of your payment is perhaps one of the most crucial factors that affect your credit score because it will indicate to lenders whether you have been disciplined in making payments on time. This is a great sign to show your probabilities of paying your future debts. As a result, even one or two payments may profoundly affect your credit score.

Dozens of skipped payments can change everything into a "derogatory mark" or "negative record" on your report. If you are only late between 30-60 days, this should not damage your score. However, if you are late for over 90 days, the credit scoring model will interpret that you are likely to repeat it. This is not a great thing because it may easily damage your credit score.

Paying bills on time is one of the best ways that you can apply to adapt and increase your credit score. Think about implementing an automatic bill payment, or installing an online alert on your accounts to monitor your bills and eliminate the risk of skipping a payment.

2. **Credit card usage**

Your credit usage is also called "debt-to-limit ratio". This ratio determines the size of your whole credit card limit. An ethical principle to follow is to ensure that your credit use ratio doesn't go past 30%. This means the lower the credit card usage, the better. When you have a higher credit card usage ratio, it will reduce your credit score and may cause prospective lenders to become scared that you may not manage more debt.

There are different methods used to reduce the credit use ratio—right from paying a debt to raising the limit on the credit.

3. **The age of the credit, and defined credit history**

A long history of credit usually changes the score as long as you have a history of making timely payments on the accounts you open.

The factors that are considered include the time the credit accounts were opened, the time specific accounts were opened, and the time elapsed since you used each account.

If you ensure that your oldest credit card remains open, it may increase your score. However, if you have a high fee to pay, it may not improve your score.

It is always a great idea to ensure that your first card is open. Closing the first credit card may affect your credit history and limit your existing credit, which may reduce your credit score.

4. Credit mix and the number of accounts active

The number of active credit accounts plays a big part in your credit score. In summary, a higher number of open credit accounts results in a better credit score. The reason is that a high percentage of your accounts implies that you are approved for credit by more lenders. Additionally, the number of open accounts, the different variety of credit across the main classifications, and the recurring installment loans and revolving credit may increase your credit score.

5. New credit and hard credit inquiries

Every time a person extracts a credit report, the insurer, lender, or landlord is listed on the credit report. There are two categories of credit inquiry:

- **Hard Inquiries:** This usually happens when a financial mortgage lender, bank, and credit company accesses a report when you register for credit. Hard inquiries are generated with permission to any individual who can generate a credit report, and this is shown on the credit score.

- **Soft inquiries:** This happens when you access a credit report but not because you are seeking new credit. When you look for a credit report copy, a soft inquiry is generated. Landlords and employers can also send a soft inquiry to deliver a customized quote.

A single hard inquiry is possibly likely to change the score by some points. However, hard inquiries can stay on the credit report for about two years, and this can destroy your score.

Why? The reason is that lenders who notice that you have many recent inquiries may be scared that you are looking at different places because you can't be eligible for the credit. Research indicates that consumers who open numerous credit accounts in a short period pose a big risk of delinquency—especially those without a long-established credit history.

What is considered a good credit score? What is a bad credit score?

So far, you must know that a credit score is a good metric of financial health. It demonstrates your level of trust to financial companies and can assist in determining how expensive and easy it can be for you to purchase a home, car, or even rent an apartment. Good credit may assist you in securing a date.

That is why it is important, if possible, to consider actions to improve your score. However, the factors that define a good or bad credit aren't broadly understood. About 25% of millennials don't understand what a good credit score is; this is based on the survey done by LendEdu.

Typically, businesses and lenders define their parameters for measuring a model they want to use and what makes up for a good score for a specific service or product. A specific score isn't an assurance for credit approval or even gets the lowest rates, but you need to focus on a better score that will increase the probability that you will get the best rates.

According to the Credit bureaus Experian, it has various score ranges, as shown below:

Credit Score	Rating	% of People	Impact
300-579	Very Poor	17%	Credit applicants may be required to pay a fee or deposit, and applicants with this rating may not be approved for credit at all.
580-669	Fair	20.20%	Applicants with scores in this range are considered to be subprime borrowers, meaning their credit standing is less than what is normally desired.
670-739	Good	21.50%	Only 8% of applicants in this score range are likely to become seriously delinquent in the future.
740-799	Very Good	18.20%	Applicants with scores here are likely to receive better than average rates from lenders.
800-850	Exceptional	19.90%	Applicants with scores in this range are at the top of the list for the best rates from lenders.

Keep in mind that the consumer percentage in each of the five credit score ranges is on average equal, and at around 20%. What makes up for "good" credit starts with a credit score of about 670. At this score level, you will qualify for approval on different loan types; this means you can have a higher rate of payment than a person with "very good" or "exceptional" credit.

Taking the right steps to boost your score can assist you in being eligible for a credit that has better rates, and also eliminate extra deposits that borrowers require when they have lower scores.

In case you see that your score isn't okay, take the time to check your credit report to see if there are any methods you can use to change your credit score over time. If you realize that your credit score is low because of inaccurate information, you can consider disputing the error.

Why your credit score is vital?

In the course of your life, there will be different times where people and businesses will depend on your score to help them decide whether you are a good fit to do business with and the types of rates you deserve. When you have a great credit score, it will provide you with many opportunities and savings. Below are some of the things that a good credit score may help you achieve:

- **Big ticket loans through traditional financial companies**

If you have been searching for a larger-sized financing option for your small business loan, your first stop may be a bank. Many people waste hours completing paperwork and gathering information for the loan application, but one of the main features of the information that plays a key part in whether you are approved for a loan or not is your credit score. This means that if you plan to get in the market for a large loan, then you will want to ensure that your credit score is in great shape. A great score will help you to qualify, and this can assist you in securing the best rates, which may lead to thousands in savings.

- **Credit cards**

Even when you have a poor credit score, it will still be easy to receive a credit card, but the options will be limited. When you have a higher credit score, you will easily qualify for various credit cards that provide customers with sign-up bonuses, entry to airport lounges, and many more. Start developing a strong credit history of timely payments so that you don't miss some of these best rewards.

- **Car financing**

For many Americans, purchasing a car is one of the best goals they can make in their life. And this can be realized when you have a good credit score. In other words, people with a good credit score have a better chance of being awarded the best rates for a car loan. Aiming to have a better credit score before you walk into the car dealership may help you save thousands of dollars in interest.

- **Online loans**

Online lenders have turned out to be the best option for traditional financial firms and are known for using technology and data to offer quick loans and make a decision on rates. Plus, they simplify the online activity. Online lenders such as Upgrade implement soft credit evaluations in case you are pre-approved for a personal loan. A strong credit score may provide you with alternative options and attractive rates of interest with online lenders.

- **Insurance**

A strong credit score and healthy credit record can assist you in earning an affordable insurance premium compared to others who have an average or poor credit record. Why? The reason is that insurance wants information that may help them to determine the risk of an applicant, and the probability that they will go delinquent on the payment of the insurance. Your credit score is a means to check risk and build a policy and premium at a cost that is in line with the level of risk they define. A great credit score may help you secure the best insurance policy at a better rate. And this will provide you and your loved ones some peace of mind.

- **Cell phone service**

One of the first things that cell phone service providers do when they want to decide whether to deliver cellular service is to confirm the history of the credit. If your credit score fails to fulfill their requirements, they might request you to make a down payment, provide you with a smaller phone selection to select from, and offer the best promotional rates. It is difficult for many people to think of life without a cell phone, but don't allow your credit score to hinder you.

- **The keys to an apartment**

Many landlords have to evaluate your credit before they can finalize the process of apartment application. For that reason, a good credit score will be advantageous from other apartment seekers in the competitive market.

How you can build your credit from scratch

Maybe you have just begun life, or maybe you have put a stop to using credit. What is the best method to build a good credit score if you don't have any at the moment?

Well, here are some strategies to try:

Look for a loan with a cosigner

- **Period**: At least six months of timely payments.

- **Level of difficulty:** It depends on your potential to get a great cosigner.

- **Who is it best for?** A person with a cosigner with high credit and ready to cosign.

This requires that you register for a loan, but look for another person to cosign the loan to convince the lender to approve it. If you don't have any credit, the loan will be created based on the history and financial potential of the cosigner.

This can go well if you are approved as a cosigner. The person may have to be ready to cosign your loan and possess the potential to qualify. If you don't have a person who can fulfill these requirements, it will not be an option.

Once you get the loan and make early payments, the lender will have to report your payment history to the credit bureaus. This will allow you to build a credit score slowly.

The drawback is that paying late affects your credit and the cosigner's credit score. In case you default, the cosigner will be asked to pay off the loan.

The best kind of loan to use this method is an auto loan. The cosigner agreements are popular with auto loans, but with an installment loan, it will generate a massive weight compared to credit cards.

Choose a "credit builder loan" – two or three

Period: Six months to one year.

Level of difficulty: Easy.

Who is it best for? A person that has at least a few hundred dollars available.

This has turned out to be a common trend in recent times, and it's present with many credit unions and banks. If you don't have a credit score, you can choose a credit builder loan, which is similar to a secured loan.

For instance, let's assume you have $500 and you want to deposit that into a savings account using a credit union. The credit union can generate a credit card using the line protected by a savings account, for around $500.

While you use the credit line and pay your monthly payments, the credit union will report the payments to the credit bureaus. Later on, they will build a credit score. This can be helpful in acquiring a second or even third credit builder loan. This will offer you multiple credit references.

With the presence of these loans, a lender can release your savings account in case you have great payment history, and the protected credit line may become unsecured. This will make it become a traditional credit card.

Become authorized to use someone else's credit card

Period: Six to twelve months.

Level of difficulty: Average because of different variables.

Who is it best for? People with less or no credit.

This method is like a mixed bag. The basic premise is that the main cardholder includes you as an authorized person to use the card. In other words, you can make charges on the card, but you aren't accountable for the payments.

This helps build a credit score, but it's subject to different aspects, and some aren't known when the arrangement is made:

- Some credit card issuers don't disclose account activity on authorized users.

- Credit scoring models may generate less weight to authorized user status, and hence, it may not feature the beneficial effect you could hope for.

- The arrangements may be helpful in case the account is in a good state. In case there are late payments by the main user, or the account balance is high, it may affect your effort, and your credit score.

- Because you aren't a primary cardholder, you may have little control over how you manage the account. This can succeed if the account is controlled, but hurt if it isn't.

Find a student credit card

Period: Six to twelve months.

Level of difficulty: Fairly simple.

Who is it best for? Students and young adults with little or no credit.

The student credit cards will allow you to start building a credit score early in life. Most provide associated services, such as information on how to control and enhance your credit.

One of the most common student credit cards is the Discover it Cash Back Card. This card provides 1% cash back on all purchases, 5% cash back on revolving purchase types, and a $20 annual bonus for better grades. The card has no annual fee and even offers you a free monthly FICO score.

To qualify for a student credit card can be challenging. If you are below 21 years of age and want to own a credit card, you will need to know how to create evidence of income to ensure you qualify for approval. You may always get approved with a part-time job. You also need to have little or no credit history without derogatory information. These cards aren't meant for people with impaired credit.

But if you can't manage to get an independent income, you will have to qualify as an authorized user on the card, with your parents as the main cardholders.

When you successfully get a student credit card, make sure that you use it responsibly. This will only assist you in growing your credit if you maintain a low balance and make timely payments. If you become sloppy and use it without any measures in place, you will perhaps have a bad credit history. And this is something that you don't want to experience in life.

Letting rent and utilities report your payment history

Period: Six to twelve months.

Level of difficulty: Depends on the strategy you use.

Who is it best for? Individuals without credit, or those that have bad credit but want to include good credit references.

Traditionally, both rent and utility payments used to work against you when it comes to credit. Neither landlords nor utility companies could reveal you have a good credit history to the credit bureaus. However, if you are aware that you have a past due balance, that will be reported to the bureaus.

Rent reporting: There are various services that one can apply to in order to get rent payments included on their credit report. Plus, unique methods on how this happens. One service includes Experian RentBureau—this will indicate your rent as a trade line, and factor in payments for the last 25 months.

The challenge is to find a landlord with whom you can report your rent history to the service. There are some charges that you need to pay, which may make the landlord reluctant. Additionally, if your landlord doesn't want to work together, you will have to begin making your rent payments to a rental collection service, which will include a certain charge. There are a wide variety of rent collection agencies, each with its own fee structure.

Another option is Rental Kharma. While this is not a rent collection service, it will still report your payment history to TransUnion. These confirm your lease and check to make sure that every payment has been made on time. You can also register for a canceled rent check for the last 24 months to assist the process along.

This kind of service will only be active if you make timely rent payments every time and every month. Luckily, many landlords will not report a late payment unless it persists for more than 30 days.

Find utility companies to report to the credit bureaus

In 2015, FICO released a new scoring model that featured utility payments. This one comprised of utility companies, as well as internet and cell phone services.

This is considered an alternative scoring model, and it applies to people who don't have a credit score. If you already have bad credit, this scoring model may not be helpful.

The other problem is the general absence of acceptance by creditors. Just a few lenders apply the FICO model. Mortgage lenders and possibly auto lenders could frequently apply it; however, its application among credit card issuers is scarce.

Alternatively, the presence of this alternative option is not included in the traditional scores of FICO.

It is possibly worth it to try it, but whether or not it's going to work will depend on your payment history using utility companies, and more importantly, whether a given lender makes use of this particular FICO score. And perhaps, if you are a student or a young person living with your parents, you will not have rent and utilities to report.

For that reason, utilities and rent have a minimum value as credit references in most situations, especially for students.

Register for credit cards for people without credit

Period: Six to twelve months.

Level of difficulty: Fairly easy.

Who is it best for? People with at least $200.

As with credit builder loans, these are protected cards. Most of these cards are offered by lenders whom you have never heard of. They operate the same style as the credit builder loans, but the credit lines are a bit smaller. Most of them have a starting credit line of $200, which may need an equal security deposit.

You'll use the cards, and pay the monthly payments, and your payment history will be sent to the credit bureaus. This will allow you to improve your credit scores slowly.

The drawback of these cards is that they have a higher fee. For instance, a lender may offer a credit limit of $200, but charge interest of $50. This will decrease your credit limit to around $150, which won't provide you much in terms of spending potential.

These cards are recommended to people who can't find a cosigner for a loan or don't have money for a credit builder loan.

The best way to boost your credit score isn't currently where you want it to be

Let's assume you already got a credit score, but it is below what you want it to be. What are some of the best means to make your credit score better?

Pay off any past debts

Period: Within 30 days.

Level of difficulty: Easier if you already have the funds; impossible if you don't.

Who is it best for? Anyone with past debts or balances.

These may comprise of due balance on active accounts, charge-offs, old debts, and tax liens.

If you have any outstanding charges, clearing them is one of the best ways you can change your credit score. Begin by first paying the smallest ones. For the big balances, enter into a negotiation with the creditor to accept less than the complete amount.

Any pay offs should comprise of a paper trail. This can be a canceled check or even a letter of satisfaction from the creditor.

However, paying off a past due balance doesn't eliminate you from the negative list from your credit report. However, a paid collection is often better than an unpaid one, so you will still be going in the right direction.

Dispute your credit errors

Period: It depends on your credit history.

Level of difficulty: It changes between moderate to more difficult.

Who is it best for? Any person with errors on their credit report.

Find a copy of your credit report, one from the top three credit bureaus. Remember that you are eligible for a free report at the end of twelve months.

Analyze the three credit reports. If you see any errors, you will have to get in touch with the reporting creditor and get the information fixed. You will possibly be required to provide documents to show the derogatory entry is a mistake. If you manage to prove your case, you will get a letter from the creditor to confirm the correction and make sure that they report it to all the three credit bureaus.

This is not an easy thing to do, but it is one of the quickest methods you can use to improve your credit scores. Any form of derogatory content you delete will increase your credit score.

However, it's important that you avoid going for a credit repair service because the reputation of members in that sector is questionable and expensive.

Make timely payments of all your obligations from now on

Period: At least twelve months, or even more.

Level of difficulty: This one will depend on your financial condition and level of commitment.

Who is it best for? Everyone.

Not only is this obvious, but you may not proceed if you aren't done with this one yet. In other words, from now onwards, pay all your monthly bills on time. And not only monthly bills, but also your debts. When talking about monthly payments, we refer to subscriptions, utilities, rent, phone services, and many more. You must develop a habit of good credit.

Track your credit from now on

Period: Ongoing.

Level of difficulty: It is easy until you find a new error.

Who is it best for? Everyone, no matter the credit level.

Once you have errors fixed, it is important to continue tracking your credit. Just like the way errors continue to show up in the past, they may continue to occur in the future. That means you will have to remain on top of this state. And that requires that you track your credit now and then.

If you are wondering how you can achieve this, a few credit score providers will assist you. One of them is Credit Karma. If you didn't know, Credit Karma is one of the most common and well known among free credit score generators. Credit Karma will provide your VantageScore3.0 from Equifax and TransUnion. They also deliver details about your credit score factors that resemble a complete credit report.

If you discover a massive drop in your score, it is probably because of some derogatory information that has been included in your credit report. You can start a dispute if the information is an error. This is often done when the error first shows up so that you have a fresh memory and required documentation is easily available.

Pay your high credit card balances

Period: Within 30 days.

Level of difficulty: Simple if you have the cash to do it, but hard when you don't.

Who is it best for? Anyone who has a high credit card balance.

Do you recall credit utilization? One of the easiest means to boost your credit scores is by cutting down your ratio and paying all your due balances. If you can bring down the ratio to 50% from 80%, the better your credit scores will be.

Apply some wonderful credit to the mix

Period: It depends on your credit history, but a minimum of twelve months.

Level of difficulty: It depends on your credit history.

Who is it best for? Everyone.

If you have a huge percentage of negative information on your credit report, you may have to counter that by applying a lot of good credit. Follow the same method as you would if you are focused on building credit scores from the start:

- Pay bills on time from this day going forward.
- Look for a credit builder loan.
- Get a consigned loan.

For bad credit, time can be your friend as long as you pay all your bills on time. A piece of derogatory credit information will disappear from your report after seven years. However, if you decide to shave off your old bad credit, and establish a pattern of good new credit, your credit scores will start to increase in less than seven years.

Easy steps to use to repair your credit and improve your credit score

Rebuilding your credit isn't that difficult, and boosting your credit score may not necessarily take months.

Fixing your credit score may generally imply qualifying for a lower interest charge and better terms. This is true regardless of whether you want a good credit score to request money for personal reasons, or you can buy inventory, and lease a facility to begin growing your business.

The issue is that credit repair is a bit like growing your professional network—you only start to think about it when it is important. However, when you don't have good credit, it becomes hard to fix the same situation overnight.

That is the reason the time to begin fixing your credit is now—before the time comes where you really need it. Luckily, it is not that hard to improve your credit score. Below are some easy processes that you can implement:

1. Dispute any late payments

Errors do happen. Your mortgage lender may send a report that a certain payment was late when in reality you paid it on time. A credit card provider may enter the wrong payment.

You are allowed to dispute these payments, whether in accounts that are current or have already been closed. It is not different from the way you challenge your derogatory marks.

Your payment profile is a great factor in your credit score, so you should remain committed to clean up the mistakes.

2. Choose whether you also want to play the games certain credit repair companies play

So far, you have learned about removing inaccurate information, but did you know that you can also decide to dispute accurate information?

For instance, let's assume that an account went to collection, you failed to pay it, and the collection entity fails to come for collection. All that is left is the record on your credit report. You can still decide to dispute this entry—many do. And there are occasions where the entries are removed.

Why? The reason is that once you start a dispute, the credit bureau will request the creditor to confirm the information. Some will, but most collection agencies don't. Instead, they ignore the request, and the agency has to clear the entry from your credit report.

In other words, smaller companies, or midsize providers, are highly likely to respond to credit bureaus. It is a task they don't need. Credit card firms, auto finance firms, banks, and mortgage lenders are highly likely to respond.

So, if you want, but this is not a recommendation, it's a method some individuals employ—you can go ahead and dispute information hoping that the creditor will not respond. This is a method that most credit repair firms use to improve the credit score of their clients. If the creditor fails to respond, the entry is omitted.

Now the question is: Should you go for this approach? That is for you to decide.

3. Make a humble request

Say you attempted to remove the derogatory comment, account marked "Paid as agreed", but failed. Should you now give up? Or give it another try?

Don't give up; you can instead make a humble request or even ask interestingly.

Creditors have the authority to allow credit bureaus to eliminate records from your credit report at any time. So when all else doesn't work, call and make a humble request. You will be surprised to learn how a humble request may assist you.

4. Increase the limits of your credit

Another important factor that plays a key role in your credit score is your credit card usage. This ratio often causes a massive change. In general, a large balance of over 50% on your existing credit will adversely affect your score. Mixing your cards will probably affect your score.

One method that you can use to ensure that you have a good ratio is to clear your balances, but another method is to increase the limit of your credit.

To have the limit/s increased, you need to call and ask politely. If you have a good payment history, most credit card companies are going to be happy to increase your limit.

Even as they increase your limit, remain disciplined so that you don't use extra available credit—if you do so, you will return to the original credit ratio boat. And you will be in big debt.

5. Open a new credit card account

You can also positively increase your credit score by choosing to open a new account. Your only goal is to make sure that there is no balance on this card, and the credit available will possibly rise depending on the limit.

Get a card that doesn't require you to pay an annual fee. Your best route has to be through a bank—of which you already have a bank account with. The cards that don't have a yearly charge tend to demand high-interest rates, but if you don't leave a balance, this may not affect you.

However, again, you need to be smart. Your target shouldn't be to have more cash but to improve the credit score. If you think you may easily use the balance on the new account, then it is better that you don't open another one.

6. Clear high-interest "new" credit accounts first

The era of credit is important to your credit report. The interest rates are important to your bank account. Let's assume you have $100 to pay down balances every month; then you must focus on clearing high-interest accounts first. Next, you can prioritize based on the age of the account. Pay the recent ones first so that you can increase the average period of the credit, which should assist you in scoring, but you will also have the ability to avoid paying off high-interest rates.

Then you can place the money that you haven't spent on that payment into another account on your list.

7. Don't throw away your old credit cards

The length of time that you have used your credit history has a moderate but useful credit score. Let's say you own a credit card for ten years. If you decide to close that account, it may reduce your general credit profile and affect your score negatively, especially in the short term.

If you are planning to raise your credit score but at the same time close your credit account, focus on closing your "newest" card.

Do it yourself credit repair: Steps to repair bad credit on your own

It is crucial that you don't fall for scams that promise easy, overnight credit repair. If you want to correct your bad credit, you can do it yourself. These simple steps will help you boost your credit score.

So far, you know that when you have poor credit, you won't qualify for new credit products, such as credit cards. Though you may manage to get an auto loan or even a mortgage, you are going to pay a high interest rate because of the poor credit score. This is unlike a person with a better credit score. Here are some potential ways to fix your credit:

1. Know where you stand

Before you start the DIY repair, you want to have complete copies of your credit reports from the three bureaus—Equifax, Experian, and TransUnion.

As mentioned, these reports are free as long as you request them once a year from www.annualcrediteport.com. Other websites may promise to grant you a free report, but that is just a lie.

2. If you get errors, dispute them

The next process in your credit repair is to file a dispute for incorrect information captured on your report. Mistakes are common, so if you see any errors, whether small or big, it is important to clear them. And here is what you need to do:

Once you receive a full copy of your credit report, verify your identity information, and your credit history.

Verify the list of credit cards, debts, and main transactions. If you notice any mistake, then you need to create a copy of the report and highlight the mistake.

Next, collect any information that you may need to provide as evidence; it could be your bank statements. This is very critical because credit bureaus will not act on anything if there is no proof.

3. Prevent the bleeding

Once you finish fixing any errors found on your credit report, this is the time to make sure that you don't spend more than what you can generate every month.

Why is this so critical? It's because there are just three simple things to do to fix a bad credit:

- Pay bills on time
- Pay your debt
- Don't apply for credit

Of course, before you can begin to do any of the listed things, you have to make sure that you don't spend more than what you earn. In other words, you must have a budget.

First, analyze the returns of your tax for the last two years to get a clue of how much money you earn at the end of the year.

Deduct your monthly expenses from your present income. Next, you need to create an estimate of how much money you spend every month on other costs, such as entertainment, gas, and groceries. After this, you should build a limit that is based on your income, and what you can spend in each of the various categories of costs.

How to get late payments deleted like the pros

Late payments cause a huge negative impact on your credit scores. If you didn't know, these payments could remain on your credit reports for seven years, so you need to do everything you can to prevent getting them.

If there are any instances of a late payment on your credit report, you will have to do something to remove it and boost your credit scores. And in case you make a late payment, there's that opportunity to have it removed.

But why do late payments appear on credit reports?

There are two reasons for this:

> 1. You aren't at fault. In this case, the late payment is a mistake.
>
> 2. You are at fault. You probably paid late.

In the first scenario, you can remove the late payment from your credit reports by filing a dispute. Credit bureaus want to have accurate information on their records, so when you file a dispute, they will look into it so they can fix the issue.

In the second instance, you may manage to get the late payment removed from the credit reports. However, this process involves applying polite language and sending a humble request. You may also need to describe your condition and promise to be disciplined and responsible in the coming years. However, this method does not guarantee that you will succeed.

Regardless of the late payment on your credit reports, it is worth it to take the time to remove it. You're going to learn when late payments will appear on your credit reports, and why it is important to remove them. Finally, you will learn how to dispute an inaccurate late payment, and how you can request lenders to wipe out records of late payments.

Point to note

When searching for credit companies to fix your credit score, you will come across multiple companies that will promise to do the service "fast" and for a price. Some may even promise to remove any negative features on your credit report. The truth is: everything these companies do, you can do it yourself; they have no special access.

While you may want to work with some of those companies, ensure that they are reputable. That way, you will save your time and energy to look for all contact details and documents to file a dispute. Instead, you can get a person who has experienced this before, and who can guide you on what to expect and speed up the whole process.

If you know that you aren't at fault, dispute the payment

As mentioned, this method is perfect if there is an incorrect late payment on your credit records that never occurred.

You can also apply this method if you did make a late payment, but there's some false information related to it. However, in this situation, you perhaps shouldn't expect a late payment record to be completely removed. But they will correct the error, and you'll still have the late payment remain there.

It is free to file a dispute of data in your credit report. You may consider disputing the late payment with various companies. Below is a basic structure:

> 1. Highlight the problem. Make sure you confirm the credit report that the late payment has shown up on.
>
> 2. Get in touch with the creditor to find out whether they will correct the error and alert credit bureaus.
>
> 3. Get in touch with credit bureaus. If it's important, get in touch with the credit bureaus to dispute late payments.

Learn to be patient. This procedure may successfully end at the second step, or it may even take longer. You don't have to experience many problems with the popular credit card issuers if they actually made an error, even if that demands that you spend a lot of time on the phone. But there is a chance that other credit card companies may be quite hard to work with, especially sub-prime cards companies.

1. Review your credit reports

If you think you may have an incorrect late payment, the first step is to verify all your credit reports to see whether it is captured on all records.

While you review your late payments, you should pay attention to the account number, lender, the amount paid, the data, and so forth.

Though this step is not that important—because credit bureaus will pull out your late payment accounts when you begin an online dispute with them—when you review your credit reports, you will have a better insight into your accounts, and when the late payment happened. And in case there is a big error on your reports, such as a late payment, it is important to check to make sure everything is accurate.

Below are some free methods to use to look at your credit reports. However, assessing your reports may not have a huge problem regarding your credit scores at all. Some of these services will provide you with comprehensive information compared to others.

1. Apply a credit monitoring service

There are different services that you can use. They don't offer you the actual credit reports, but they can display the information the reports have. Some of those services include:

- Credit.com for Equifax and TransUnion reports.

- CreditKarma for the Experian and TransUnion reports.

- Experian free membership. This is meant for little information related to your Experian report.

- Capital One CreditWise for the TransUnion report.

- The Chase Credit Journey meant for TransUnion reports.

i) You can visit AnnualCreditReport.com to receive a free copy of your credit report per year.

ii) You may qualify for extra free credit reports.

2. Dispute the lender

Once you note that there is a false late payment on one or more of your credit reports, then it could be time to get in touch with the lender who sends the report.

If they are a credit card issuer, it will be easy as calling the number written on the back of your card, or reviewing the list of credit company contact details. If not, you may have to look for the right contact information to call the lender.

You may be lucky to succeed in calling and alerting them to the error. They may review their records, and identify the mistake, and take the necessary steps to correct it.

In some cases, the lender could ask for a request to show proof that you didn't make any late payment. They may even ask for a letter that has a copy of a bank statement indicating the payment, or any form of documentation. If they are satisfied, they will fix the error.

When the lender accepts that the late payment is an error, it is important to put it in writing. Find a written verification that shows the late payment reporting error from the lender, and not your mistake.

Next, ask the lender to file a dispute of the late payment with the credit agencies and have it purged out from your credit report. If they can't dispute it, then you may have to do it on your own.

Regardless of whether the lender will send the dispute or you will do it on your own, you have to make sure that you review your reports after every month so that you can verify the late payment is fixed.

Another thing that the lender has to do once it is proven that it's an error is to refund any late payments that you made.

The lender may accept that it was an error, but that doesn't imply that the late payment will instantly vanish from your reports. In particular, when the lender doesn't file for disputes with the credit bureaus, you will have to implement this step by yourself.

If you fail to show that you made payments on time, you may be unfortunate. But still, you can go ahead and start a dispute with the credit bureaus if you are sure the late payment is a mistake.

3. Disputing with the credit bureaus

Disputes can be done online, or even via mail or cell phone. When you file a dispute for an item on your credit report, the credit bureau has to launch an investigation that may take longer. The bureau will have to analyze the information and confirm with the lender if it is necessary. Once they prove that the item is correct, it will have to remain on the credit report. If they find that the item is incorrect, they will remove it from your report.

Keynote

If you make a late payment, don't file a dispute as inaccurate. Some people attempt this, hoping to get some luck when the creditor fails to verify in time. This is making false claims and may destroy your relationship with the credit card issuer, and they may fail to approve you for cards in the future.

It is advised that you dispute online; that way, it will be faster, and more accurate. Every credit bureau has a free online dispute system that you can apply to.

If you dispute through email, make sure that you send the information listed below. This could be really helpful even though it looks too much:

- A copy of your utility bank, bill, or insurance statement.
- Your date of birth.
- Your Social Security Number.
- An address to show where you have lived in the last two years.
- Your full names.
- Any supportive documentation, such as a notice from the lender that the late payment is inaccurate, or even a bank statement to indicate the timely payment.

Make sure you send copies of documents, and not the original versions because you won't get them back. You don't have to write a long, detailed explanation of your condition; however, the more evidence you provide, the better.

You are the one at fault

If you know that you made a late payment, you still have a chance to have it purged from your credit report. This may be a slim opportunity, but it is important to try because a late payment has a major impact on your credit.

These methods require you to contact the creditor, instead of the credit bureaus. You will basically be pleading your case and requesting them to pardon you the late payment. The creditors have no condition to do so. If they choose to report the account as current rather than a delinquent, this is often referred to as "goodwill adjustment".

This may succeed if you do have a great payment history with the lender, and you have been a disciplined customer except for this single mistake. If a technical error hindered you from paying on time—for example, a problem with the payment system—that may work to your favor. Or, say there was a massive life event that hindered you from paying on time, they could be sympathetic to that.

If you haven't been a great customer, and you have a history of late payments plus other negative comments, you may not have much success with the "goodwill adjustment". However, it could be worth trying it based on your condition because it will not cost you anything.

You have only two steps for the following process:

    1. Ask nicely

    2. Negotiate

Goodwill adjustment using a phone call or letter

You can attempt a goodwill adjustment using two methods: mail and phone. Some people only try one, while some attempt both. Typically, many people tend to have success from calling and sending multiple letters over time, but this cannot be confirmed.

Whether you are on the phone or you write a letter, keep in mind that you are at fault here and it is important to ask for forgiveness. The tone you speak with should reflect that too. Be thankful, polite, and conscientious. Besides this, don't get demanding or angry.

Below are some examples to help you start a phone conversation or a goodwill letter. If you do find a positive response from the creditor, you should try to get it in writing.

Phone

Use the script below to begin a conversation about clearing your late payment. Just confirm that you have your explanation for why you were late. If you don't have a great payment history, you may have to adjust it gradually to reveal your initial state.

LATE PAYMENT GOODWILL ADJUSTMENT SAMPLE PHONE SCRIPT

"Hello, my name is [your name]. I recently made a late payment on my account, which was a total accident.

As you can see, my payment history is perfect other than this one mistake. I ended up paying late because [insert your explanation here]. The late payment is also showing up on my credit reports.

Is there any way you could remove this late payment from the record, by reporting that account as always current?"

This should get you started in the right way.

Mail

Take the time to write a great, old-fashioned letter. A goodwill letter has to be customized to reflect the current situation and the good intention to be a disciplined credit user.

Accept your mistake for the late payment, and don't make excuses. Explain some of the conditions surrounding it, whether it was about your potential to pay, some confusion, or some other reason. Highlight that you have been making other payments on time. If there is something that hindered you from a timely payment, explain that it's not a problem now.

The sample letter below should work as a great template to get you started. Make sure you adjust it where possible to fit your condition.

LATE PAYMENT GOODWILL ADJUSTMENT SAMPLE LETTER TO CREDITOR

[Date]
[Your Name]
[Your Address]
[Your Phone Number]
[Your Email Address]
[Your Account Number]

Complaint Department
[Name of Creditor]
[Creditor Address]

Dear Sir or Madam,

I hope you're doing well today. My name is [your name], and I've been a satisfied customer of [creditor] for [number] of years. I've always made my payments on time, but unfortunately I recently made a mistake on [date].

I understand how important it is to make timely payments. However, I missed my payment because [brief explanation of why you missed your payment]. But I'm confident this won't happen again. As you can see from my credit history, I have a long record of on-time payments before and since the late payment.

As a courtesy, I respectfully request that you make a goodwill adjustment to remove the late payment on [date]. Please consider my track record as proof that I take my financial obligations seriously.

If you have any questions, or if you would like to speak with me in more detail, please call me at [your phone number] or send me an email at [your email address here].

Thank you for your consideration.

[Your name]

Try to negotiate

If a regular goodwill adjustment fails to deliver the expected results, you can attempt to negotiate. You could have some leverage to work with, but maybe not.

There are different types of offers that you could make:

- *Autopay:* This is where you set up an automatic payment system so that the creditor can receive timely payment.

- *Payment plan:* You need to agree to pay a given amount each month to pay off a current balance.

- *Partial settlement:* This one requires you to pay the outstanding balance, and agree to pay off the rest over time.

- *Complete settlement:* Pay off the remaining balance with the creditor.

Attempt any negotiating technique that you know; you may be lucky if you can demonstrate that you're financially able to make the payment every month.

To include the negotiation technique in your phone call or goodwill letter, you only need to insert one of these scripts into the conversation. Or you can combine them in a certain way.

AUTOPAY

On my part, I'll sign up for the autopay system so you can be sure that you'll always get my payments on time. I have a good job with a steady income, so I'm not worried about missing future payments.

PAYMENT PLAN

On my part, I'll pay off my remaining balance of [your account balance] over the next [number of months] months, making payments of [payment amount] each month. I'll sign up for autopay so you can be sure that you'll always get my payments on time. I have a good job with a steady income, so I'm not worried about missing future payments.

PARTIAL SETTLEMENT

On my part, I'll pay [payment amount] of my outstanding balance now, and will pay off the rest over the next [number of months] months. I'll sign up for the autopay system so you can be sure that you'll always get my payments on time. I have a good job with a steady income, so I'm not worried about missing future payments.

FULL SETTLEMENT

On my part, I'll pay off my entire balance of [your account balance] now to show my commitment. I intend to remain a loyal customer. I have a good job with a steady income, so I'm not worried about missing future payments.

How to find Credit cards with guaranteed approval?

If you have been struggling to get a credit card because you already have bad credit, you may be asking yourself about the guaranteed approval card offers you have seen. Are they genuine? And what exactly does guaranteed approval really mean? Although this term may seem like the solution to your credit card problems, the truth is that all credit cards have certain basic requirements before a company can release one to you. One key thing with the guaranteed approval is that there are minimum requirements set for one to qualify.

Many issuers of guaranteed approval require a person to have an active checking account and to show evidence of income that it surpasses a specific minimum amount. There is also the issue of how bad your credit is. In general, a credit score of between 300 and 650 is bad credit. But some card issuers will view a score of 550-650 as poor credit, and they may consider you for an unsecured credit card.

The process of signing up for guaranteed approval credit cards is done online. These credit cards will provide you with immediate approval. Also, they are meant for people with bad credit.

For those that have bad credit, it is easy to be deceived by these offers. However, before you move forward and sign up, consider the following tips:

1. Don't submit many applications

Don't send multiple applications for guaranteed approval. This may damage your credit.

2. Have a repayment plan

When you are approved, do you have an effective repayment plan? Don't get into a state of being unprepared. The best thing to recall as a credit card holder is to stay up to date with your bills no matter the type of credit card you have. Will your monthly income let you pay additional expenses? Or it is practical to improve your credit first before you receive a credit card?

3. Plan for other options

When you have different options, it will help you increase the score of your credit card. Some of these options include a department store and gas station card. It is easy to get these cards, and they do the same work as credit cards.

4. Be ready to pay off your balance completely

If you choose to own a bad credit card, you have to be ready to fulfill your obligations of paying for it. Don't let anything discourage you from paying your credit card debts. Make sure that you note down your payment dates.

5. Read before signing

This is very important; you need to read each statement found on the terms and conditions of your credit card. Be sure that you have understood everything. If there are questions, don't be afraid to call the bank and speak to a representative. It is important to be confidently aware that you don't have hidden charges or vague clauses in your credit card.

Chapter 2: Paying Off debt

Lies about Debt

Today's society has spread a bunch of lies about the debt that we have come to believe as true. Some of us have believed them to the point where many of us are already in debt.

But how can we stop believing these lies and start to dwell on the truth? One way is by educating ourselves and learning what debt is and what it is not.

Many different lies have been propagated about debt. Let's take a look at some of them:

1. Find a credit card to build your credit

This perception that you have to look for a credit to grow credit implies that you have to have debt so that after some time you can increase your debt. It is ridiculous. The idea of purchasing a home later on emerges. So, can you get a house without a credit card? The lenders will say no, but this is not true.

You can get a mortgage from a firm that is involved in underwriting. This means that you don't just focus on your credit score but look at your financial history. You may be eligible for mortgages if you have paid your bills on time for the last two years, have a great history of paying your utilities on time, or have been in the same career for a minimum of two years, and have an excellent record of payment.

You may think this is very difficult—only because someone told you about an alternative route. The truth is that you don't need to apply for credit to purchase a home. An excellent history of financial stewardship will help you get a home when the time comes to buy one.

2. All debt is bad

This negative perception associated with debt has caused a large number of people to begin thinking that all debt is bad. While irresponsible borrowing isn't a great thing, a well-handled debt can become positive and assist you in building your credit history and enhancing your credit score.

This will increase the credit score to boost your chances of getting credit in the future and securing big loans such as mortgages.

Also, a mortgage can be said to be good debt because it aids in getting a long-term investment.

3. Debt consolidation repairs our issues with debt

Debt consolidation is a significant issue because it hides a huge problem. From a purely financial standpoint, it may look like a great idea; however, the challenge is that we are the ones who drive ourselves into debt. We are the architects of our problems. And so, when we decide to consolidate our debts, we may start to think like we have done something to repair the problem. We feel we have achieved something, but the fact is that nothing has changed. The debt will still stand, and nothing shall have changed; we are the same.

Debt is a fundamental issue. It includes impatience, poor financial management, and impulse buying. To fix this problem, you have to review yourself further than the amount of debt. Consolidating the loans doesn't change anything; it is like transferring the problem from one party to another. If you want to see a permanent long-term change that will affect your future finances, then it is crucial to fix individual habits that led to the debt.

Just because everyone is doing it doesn't mean that you need to do it. The fact is that you don't need to get a credit card to grow your credit. Car loans aren't the ticket to a better life, and you can't repair your debt problem by consolidating it. By rejecting these lies and trying to live in a disciplined and responsible manner, you will prepare yourself for success and finally achieve complete financial freedom.

4. That you can declare bankruptcy

It is the last thought that many people often think about—that when the business fails, or your student loan debt grows beyond your abilities, bankruptcy is the last option. It is not the choice that most people want, but it is there as an exit route.

However, it's even hard to accomplish these responsibilities when you have declared bankruptcy. This is especially true when you have some reasonable household income.

The fact is that before you can file for bankruptcy, you have to fulfill several requirements before you are discharged for bankruptcy. Also, you may have to demonstrate that you are insolvent rather than able to pay off your debt after some time.

5. Debt advice is expensive

While certain debtors will ask you for some fee before giving you advice, many expert firms and organizations will offer advice free of charge. The consulting charities plus debt management firms can assist you in gaining knowledge of debt options.

6. Having debt is a bad thing

Despite the perception of debt, as a borrower, you need not be ashamed of borrowing, especially when you know you are doing it wisely. Mortgages will allow you to stay in a home that will probably increase in value, and student loans will provide you with methods to invest in yourself.

By choosing to use credit cards, you will get the chance to demonstrate that you can borrow responsibly, and pay all your bills on time, and by doing so, you will be increasing your credit score. A high credit score will also make financial organizations feel secure to lend you more money, and you may even qualify for big loan terms and attractive rates of interest.

Similarly, non-creditors, such as home insurers, electric utilities, landlords and cell phone companies, may also be interested to see your credit score. However, remember that when you constantly have a specific amount of credit card debt compared to your line amounts, it may negatively affect your credit score.

7. Maintaining a credit card balance will increase your credit score

This is another misconception. One way to improve your credit score is to use a small size of your credit, making sure that you pay all your bills on time every month.

8. Retail credit cards are a good thing

Not really. You need to read the part that talks about when you carry the balance of a previous month to the next month. The retail credit cards can be very attractive, especially when you are given free interest and rewards; however, when you carry the balance of this month into the next month, things start to fall apart fast. Some cards are similar to payment plans, where borrowers will buy a card from retailers, and then pay it after some months with "interest-free"; however, when you fail to clear the whole balance within the quoted period, you will perhaps pay interest on the entire amount, and at a higher interest rate than a normal credit card. For instance, Apple provides customers with an eighteen-month interest-free option when you use Barclaycard US card to make purchases. However, if you fail to pay off the purchase in the interest-free time, a variable yearly rate percentage is implemented. Your history isn't that important; whether you have a great credit history or not, you may easily find yourself paying an interest of 20%.

9. It is wise to throw away credit cards that you don't use

Probably not; in fact, you need to maintain old cards that have no balances and use them a little to ensure that they remain active. The reason extends to your credit score, and an aspect applied is computation, referred to as "credit utilization rate".

10. Once you are married, you are responsible for your spouse's debt

Most couples think that once they are married, the debts merge, but this is not the case. It is popular for couples to pay off debts together, but no spouse is bound to pay off the debt of his or her life partner.

There are methods in which security may be lost once they get married; however, you can be accountable for the debt your spouse applies if you include your name on the promissory note.

11. Debts are cleared after six years

Unfortunately, there is no way a debt can be cleared if you haven't paid it. Even if it is going to last ten years, the records will remain to show that you need to pay a specific amount for a given debt. This misconception tends to be propagated by graduates.

12. Consumer proposals are a bad thing to handle debt

This is yet another big misconception spread about debt. Well, consumer proposals have some drawbacks; however, they serve a certain purpose and are usually applied when debt rises to unmanageable heights.

And the reason why consumer proposals have bad perception is that personal finance bloggers usually hit out on them, simply because personal finance advocates living a debt-free life. However, a consumer proposal isn't meant for normal debt reduction. Consumer proposals assist people when they have a massive amount of debt. If living frugal and creating a budget doesn't reduce your debt, then consumer proposal could turn out to be the most reasonable choice.

They are also acceptable and legal to handle huge sums of debt and offer an alternative to bankruptcy. It is a minimum measure, and when structured in the right way, it can be a handy option. You need to know that handling debt becomes a problem when you have to come up with a plan to control your money and develop your credit rating.

13. Bankruptcy affects a credit score extensively such that you can't be approved for credit again.

Not true. If you are planning to file for bankruptcy, your credit score is already poor from the late payments and large amounts of debts. Declaring bankruptcy may not affect your score the way you think. Fair Isaac Corporation says that if you have a score of about 680, then bankruptcy may reduce it by 130-150 points. This is an approximation. It is hard to predict the exact effects. Even when your credit score drops, you may still qualify for a line of credit. Many lenders have stopped to consider bankruptcy as a deal breaker when they approve and deny credit applications. Bankruptcy can help free some of your salaries so that you can pay for future debts. Keep in mind too, that bankruptcy isn't permanent; it is removed from your credit report after seven to ten years.

14. Paying debts will immediately repair your credit report

False. A credit report will show you a summary of your current credit standing and your credit history. Much negative information remains on your credit report for either seven or more years. By clearing your debts, it will help increase your credit report and credit score, but it will not clear all past problems. It requires time.

15. You need to pay off the mortgage as fast as possible

This is false only when considered in a one-size-fits-all form. Mortgages have a massive debt, and clearing them away may remove a major factor of stress and financial problems, especially when you are close to retiring.

Rushing to pay off your mortgage isn't the right option for everyone. Some of the things that you need to think about include:

- Is it better to invest the money on additional payments?
- Are the tax benefits that come with the mortgage interest deduction significant to you?
- Will retiring your mortgage early imply that you need to sacrifice other crucial things, such as paying off your credit card balances every month?

16. You can budget away out of debt

There is a significant difference between the financial crisis and debt.

Many people with huge debts have probably overspent their income. Credit became a means to fulfill their lives. And today they have 30K in debt, and have to work hard, earn extra, and begin a debt snowball.

That said, there's a massive difference in the way you can overcome debt and the way you can go through a financial crisis. For certain individuals, the most comprehensive budget and extreme lifestyle cut may not solve the issue of income because it cannot fulfill the fixed costs and debts payments.

The fact is that debt can turn out to become a financial crisis, and this is where many people lack the experience to handle high amounts of debt.

This is the point where you find someone losing their home. This is the time when a lawsuit begins. This is where savings are cashed out, insurance payments come to a standstill, and bankruptcy comes to mind.

The good debt versus bad debt

Before you make that final step to borrow money, it is important to understand the difference between what is considered good debt and what is said to be bad debt. Some debts are worth it; others can infect you with a financial crisis.

Some people find it hard to live debt free—at least they will have some debt to pay off. While some debts are discouraged, good debt is considered as the money you borrow so that you can pay for things that you really need or things that increase in value. On the flip side, bad debt is one that arises from things that you only want and often decrease in value.

So that you can understand the difference between good debt and bad debt, you need to know the difference between wants and needs. Before you can borrow money, you have to decide whether the money is going to do something that will have a negative and positive effect on your general financial condition.

Of course, debt isn't a bad thing; it's just how you use the money that matters.

For a good debt, you will always have a good reason to justify it, and a developed plan for paying it so that you can clear the debt as quickly as possible.

An individual with good debt will also have the cheapest methods of borrowing money. They will do this by looking at the borrowing method, rate of interest, credit amount, and charges that are appropriate to them.

Sometimes, it may imply a deal with the least possible interest rate, but sometimes, it may not.

Examples of good debt

1. Paying for medical care

There is no fixed amount of money to borrow to ensure your loved one stays healthy. You can manage to pay off the money you borrow, but it is impossible to replace a human life. If a person requires expensive treatments to ensure they remain healthy, this would be an acceptable debt, no matter what.

2. Borrow money for education

When you apply for a student loan debt, you aren't making a wrong decision. In general, people with college degrees earn more income in their life than those without a degree.

And applying for a student loan so that you can support the education of your child defeats the idea of using your savings. After all, you cannot borrow money to pay for your savings. Multiple government programs provide low-interest student loans, and you can always cut student loan interest on your taxes.

3. Taking out a mortgage on a home

Taking a loan of this amount can be overwhelming, but purchasing a house creates ownership in something that will house you, and generate some retirement money. Even while you struggle to clear your debt, you may consider it an advantage to put any available liquid cash as a deposit, though it may not be the right choice.

A home mortgage interest is cut on your taxes, and the rate of interest is lower on your home loan than on the credit card. In other words, it is important to have money to pay for other expenses instead of credit.

Though purchasing a house was initially considered a strong, future-proof investment, certain homeowners do find themselves on the wrong side on their home mortgage loan. They owe banks more than the value of their homes. However, strategic planning, purchasing only what you can afford, and maintaining low interest by having good credit may allow you to purchase a home that one day you will own completely.

4. Buying a car

If you don't have public transport in your area, or you cannot manage to get someone with whom you can carpool with, then you may have to consider buying a car. An auto loan can either be "good" or "bad", but the main thing is to ensure that the auto loan is a good debt, so look for the lowest possible rates on your loan. In addition, you need to make a large down payment while ensuring that you remain with some cash on hand just in case you need it.

Your best goal should be to go for a used car model instead of a brand-new one, possibly saving yourself thousands on the sticker price and the interest that is paid throughout the loan.

5. Business loans

While this may not be seen as good debt, borrowing money to begin a business or expand a business is perhaps a great idea if the business is thriving. After all, you need money to make more money, right?

Sometimes, you may have to borrow capital to employ new people, purchase a new device, pay for advertisement, or even develop the first new widget you designed. The point is that you borrow this money to expand the business or increase income, then this will count as good debt.

What is bad debt?

Bad debt is that which depletes your wealth and isn't affordable. Plus, it provides no means to pay for itself.

Bad debts may have no realistic repayment plans and usually deplete when people buy things at an impulse. If you aren't sure whether you can repay the money, then don't borrow the money because that will be a bad debt.

Examples of bad debt

   1. The credit card debt

A typical household in the United States has a balance of more than $10,000 on their credit card every month. However, the debt usually increases faster than we may realize and is always used to purchase things that we want instead of need. It is easier to think that you can afford something using a card than paying it with cash.

By the time you pay for your credit card, the interest rates of $100 items can be $200, and most items depreciate quickly—this makes the loss significant. In other words, credit card debt is a form of bad debt and one in which millions of Americans are using today. It is tough to pay off your credit card debt, and that is why it is better to avoid it in the first place.

   2. Borrowing from a 401K

When you ask for money from a 401K program, you will need to chat with the IRS, and if you aren't using the money to purchase a home, you will need to pay the loan in five years. If you fail to pay it back, you risk being charged with a severe penalty. Also, the interest that you pay on the loan will get taxed twice.

You can't get a loan to fund your retirement. For that reason, borrowing money from your retirement plan to use it to pay for anything that isn't part of retirement is a bad idea. You will be putting your retirement at risk when you get a loan from a 401k, so don't make this mistake.

   3. Payday loans

It may appear easy to borrow money from payday loan firms, but it is hard to pay it back. These companies offer loans with very high interest rates. The companies take advantage of the fact that many people need that money. As a result, borrowing a small amount may end up costing you a lot.

Payday loans aren't considered the worst kind of debt that you can take on. If you really need a short-term loan, it is better to go for a cash advance on a credit card rather than borrow money from these firms.

4. Jewelry, expensive clothes, and vacations

If you can't afford to pay for these luxuries using real cash, then don't do it. These are not needs but wants, and that means they are bad debt. Wait until the time when you have money to pay for them. By running into debt so that you can go for a vacation is perhaps a terrible use of money.

In summary, modern life demands many of us to borrow money at one point; however, learning the difference between good debt and bad debt can make a huge difference in your financial health and opportunity for success.

It is better not to get into more debt that you will struggle to pay back, whether it is good or bad. In addition, don't let debt accrue to more than 36% of your total gross income because credit agencies can't distinguish between a good and bad debt when calculating your credit score. If you find yourself having many debts, then you will need to search for ways to reduce your debt and get back on track.

Don't let debt scare you; instead, use it as a means to improve your life or financial condition, invest in your future, or increase your earnings.

Steps to pay back your debts fast

Paying off all your debt isn't easy, but it is possible, even if you have the least amount of money, no properties, and no idea of how to begin. Whether you are struggling with credit cards or mortgage loans, these steps will help you get out of debt fast, regardless of whether you are dead broke:

Step 1: Know how much debt you need to pay back

You may not believe the amount of money people throw away by skipping this first step and paying bills blindly without taking a more in-depth look.

This narrows down to the fact that people have a negative attitude towards debt. They consider debt as a big crime and shame in their life. And so, they feel guilty about their debt. When feeling this way, you will never want to think about how much debt you need to pay; in fact, some prefer to bury their heads in the sand than confront the reality of the situation.

This is basically what credit and loan companies look forward to. They want to hide from you the statement, and then you send them the minimum payment knowing that you have cleared all your debt. They enjoy it when you do it that way.

What you need to learn today is that the minimum payments drain your pocket more.

It can be hurtful to learn the truth by yourself, but you have to swallow the pill. From this point, you can learn that it is not hard to avoid this habit; in fact, credit card companies can assist you. Find your credit card and call the number at the back, and ask them for the debt you owe, the APR, and minimum monthly payment.

This is the time to step up and accept your debt. You either choose to do the hard work now or suffer doing the impossible later.

Luckily, this chart will help you achieve that.

How much debt do you have?

Name of credit card	The total amount of debt	APR	Monthly minimum payment

This table will help you know how much you need to pay for every company, and the interest rates.

Now stop and do this.

Have you done so?

Congratulations! Implementing the first step is always the most challenging. Now you are on your way to becoming debt free.

If the total number of debt appears high, consider the following things:

>1. There are many people with more debt than you.

>2. From today that number is going to reduce. This is the start of the end.

>Now that you know how much you owe, what next?

Step 2: Chose your "strategy of attack" for clearing the debt

>Once you know the exact amount of debt, you are ready to begin working on your debt. To achieve this, you have to organize the type of debts you're going to pay first. Whether you want to pay student loans, a credit card—whatever depending on your choice.

>To fully pay off all your debt, you may have to start with the loan that has the highest interest rate.

>For instance, assume credit card A has a balance of $1,000 and a 12% interest rate, whereas credit card B has $1,500 and

6% interest. You channel $150 per month by paying the minimum payment (3%) on one and the remaining amount on the other. This means you will save a lot of money by clearing credit card A ($147 interest) compared to card B ($188).

When you decide what you want to start with first, the next thing is to develop the plan of attack.

For student loans, you can probably save thousands of dollars every year, and pay down your debt more each month.

Yes. You can save money by spending MORE.

Assume you have $10,000 as a student loan, and the interest rate is 6.8 %, with a ten-year period to complete the payment.

If you apply the standard monthly plan, you will have to pay $115 per month.

But can you find out how much you can save every year if you simply paid $100 more every month?

Monthly payments	Total interest paid	You save
$115	$3,810	$0
$215	$1,640	$2,169
$315	$1,056	$2,754
$415	$782	$3,027

As mentioned, paying the least amount is more expensive. Even $30 per month can save you lots of money.

Step 3: Time to freeze your credit card debt—to stop it from growing

If you ever wanted to pay off all your debts, you have to learn to reduce your debt. That is the reason why this step requires you to implement these things:

1. Find your wallet.
2. Get all your credit cards.

3. Send them by mail to a different location.

Well, perhaps you don't need to go this extreme… but this makes you see the main point, which is to eliminate all temptation of wanting to use the credit card/s. You can only think of using it once you are debt free.

Here is a great tip that may work for you: throw all your cards into a basin of water and plunge them all into your freezer. If you can freeze your credit, you may need to insert your hands through a huge block of ice for you to get it back. This provides you with the time to decide whether or not you want the thing that you planned to buy.

Similarly, you can put all your credit cards in a safe, or whomever you trust to keep them for you. The point is that you aren't supposed to increase your credit card debt.

Step 4: Use this template to negotiate

Many people aren't aware of this, but it can help you save more than $900 in interest if you learn tips of negotiation.

Using negotiation tips, you can manage to limit the APR on your credit card and generate thousands of bucks.

Step 5: Make use of your "hidden income" to pay off your extra $1,000 + /month

If you have come to this point, you could be saying, "This is nice and all, but where do I find the money to pay the bills?"

Here are four recommended things:

1. Utilize the cash you have made from Step 4.

2. Make use of the money you have earned from a Conscious Spending Plan.

3. Get deeper into hidden income.

4. Earn a lot of money.

Secrets to getting out of debt

Debt can bog you down and makes it difficult for a person to live a great life. If you are tired of struggling to pay your debt, here are some secrets to help you get out of debt:

1. Daydreaming can assist you to get out of debt

Daydreaming is a great way to come out of debt. Obviously, you don't want to spend your entire time fantasizing, but if you can spend some minutes imagining your credit card balance/s at zero, it can do wonders.

Mindful meditation can help reduce your blood pressure and allow you to develop a positive mindset about clearing debt; this can be useful in taking the right action.

2. Say no to late charges—and this will increase your opportunities of getting out of debt

The amount of cash that is pumped into the late charges can damage your efforts to clear your debt. If possible, you can put an end to paying late fees. If maintaining a track of when your bills will be due is hard, then you need to consider using an app such as Check, which will notify you when it is the correct time to pay.

3. Confirm your balances every day

This may appear to be overkill, but it's not. Quick reminders should be your best bet to get out of debt. If you only check your balances once per month when you pay your bills, after a few days, the truth of your debt may start to disappear in your mind. Then when a spending chance comes up, you are likely to bite and drive yourself into more debt.

Every day when you rise, take the time to review your debt condition. By seeing it the way it is, you will be encouraged to stick to your budget, and look at your debt getting cleared.

4. Declare your plans to get out of debt

Talk to your friends and family about your plans for clearing the debt. Tell them to keep on asking about your debt.

5. Plan to become a one-car household

If you have two cars, plan on eliminating one and walk while you go to work or carpool. You may be surprised to learn that these little habits can save you thousands every year by using a single car. The average vehicle owner does spend more than $9,000 annually to maintain their vehicle.

6. Have two jobs to help pay down your debt fast

Finding a second job, or regularly selecting an extra shift or two, is a quick way for people to clear their debt; however, this strategy doesn't apply to everyone, but if you can succeed to make it work, you may free yourself from debt within a few years. For this to occur, you need to use all your additional income to pay your debt. Working extra hours doesn't have to be permanent—once you have cleared your debts, you can consider scaling back again.

You can also think about building an extra income to clear your debt by taking advantage of a hobby you like, or even a skill set that you like. For instance, if you know how to write, you can try out freelancing for newspapers, media outlets, and blogs on freelance sites. If you enjoy crafting, you can think about selling your work on Etsy. If you are good at handy work, you may look for a site which will help you link up with people who require extra skills.

Some people even use their homes to make extra cash. Can it be possible for you also to rent your storage space in your garage, or even rent your house on Airbnb?

7. Refinancing your mortgage

If you have a mortgage, you might have sufficient equity to merge all your mortgage debts. If you don't have enough equity in your house, extra mortgage costs may be expensive. Just ensure that you review all the options and look for advice from a different person besides your lender. If a normal bank isn't enough to assist you, don't be quick to look for the first home equity finance firm that is ready to provide you money. However, you should engage in a conversation with a certified, non-profit credit counselor first. You might have great options apart from refinancing your house that you aren't aware of. They can assist you in reviewing all the options available and developing the best plan to drive you forwards and fulfill your financial goals.

If you succeed in refinancing your house and merge debts into your mortgage, you may have to start thinking of a new mortgage. It is very important that you ensure your spending is within your income. Having a budget that you follow is the best way to do this and assign cash to every monthly saving. If you fail to save money, you could be tempted to ask for more when "emergencies" emerge.

8. Avoid paying retail

Make it your goal to get out of debt and avoid paying a complete price. Always go for a bargain for all your purchases, and if you don't get a deal on brand names, generics are another option.

You can save huge income that can be channeled to clearing debt by asking price comparisons, shopping sales, and store coupons that are found through smartphone apps.

9. Have accounts at two different banks

Divide and conquer works magically when you want to pay off your debt. Allocate enough money into your daily checking account to deal with daily and monthly expenses. Get a different account to contribute your debt money, like an online bank.

Avoid carrying the debit card for a debt account so that you don't use the money for daily purchases. Pay off your debt from that account alone.

Using the law of attraction to come out of debt

If you positively think about becoming debt free, then the "law of attraction" can help you realize your goals. You may be asking yourself whether you only need to think positively as the only method to pay off your debt, or even asking whether the law of attraction is a practical means to avoid debt accumulation?

Whether this is going to be your first encounter with the law of attraction, or you have been practicing it before, the secret is that it will help you develop the right mindset to become debt free.

Keep in mind that everything in the world is energy. Each element in the world has its unique vibrational energy. Humans have a vibrational frequency, money has a vibrational frequency, and even debt has a vibrational frequency. While you match the vibrational frequency of objects, you will be drawing them nearer to you.

If you have debt, then you have to match the vibrational frequency of the debt. You may still need to change the vibrational frequency so that it can be the same with being debt free, and match the money frequency.

How to change your vibrational frequency

1. The thoughts

There is a high probability that you spend a good amount of time thinking about the debt you have. You could be wondering how and when you will manage to clear it. This is the worst thing to do because you will be drawing a lot of debt to you. Every time these thoughts come to you, you will be changing your vibration to the one of being in debt.

All your thoughts are normally self-fulfilling. The process of thinking you are in debt results in you applying the law of attraction to stay in debt.

Stop concentrating on debt, and begin thinking about what you want to attain—financial security, freedom, excellent credit, and sufficient money to buy whatever you want.

You also need to stop concentrating on the debt that you have because it can discourage you.

2. Your feelings

Did you know that your feelings can create?

Yes, your feelings can show what you are building in life at any time. Your feelings will allow you to implement the law of attraction to come out of debt.

When feeling good, you will be on your way to becoming debt free. A lot of money and opportunities will come to you to pay off the debt.

You can't assume that you'll feel better once you become debt free. You need to feel good at this moment so that the law of attraction can relieve you from debt. First, feel good, and things will become better.

When you are overwhelmed or even disappointed, you can see all kinds of problems. When you feel happy, joyful, and uplifted, you will see the opportunities and steps you can make to change your debt.

3. Heart energy

This is a powerful method to use to get out of debt fast. The method requires you to send heart energy to every individual you owe money to.

Send it to every person who works at your credit card company and bank.

Send it to every person at the store when you buy clothing, groceries, and much more.

Look at each bill that is brought to you because you are surrounded by heart energy.

The most important thing is to send the heart energy to money that comes to you. It will attract money to you like a magnet.

4. Celebrate

This is the time to start celebrating when you make it. Whether it is jumping up and down in happiness, or even thanking yourself, enjoy that your debt is paid off.

Enjoy the little success that you experience as you pay off each debt, and start to get your head above water.

You will be changing your vibration to one where you are debt free every time you do so. It is simple to apply the law of attraction to jump out of debt.

Where to find money

If you struggle to clear your credit card balances, you may have to consider alternative ways—if possible, a side hustle to make some extra cash. If you don't know places that you can turn to for extra income, don't worry; you can make money online using the least amount of effort.

Let's look at some of the methods you can apply to make money online:

1. Mechanical Turk

If you want to generate some money doing little tasks, Mechanical Turk can be the best way to go. Amazon powers this site, and it allows clients to post simple tasks with short instructions, including transcriptions, surveys, audio recordings, and many more. Most of these tasks pay a little amount of cash, but the task is easy to complete. Plus, it takes a short time, and the sign-up process is quick and easy.

2. eBay

This is a great site to make some passive income. Here, you can sell anything that you want, and generate some extra money to pay your debts. It doesn't need much effort; you simply get products or even create products that you believe people will enjoy purchasing. Once you have ideas about the things you want to sell, you will realize that you can make more cash, and pay all your monthly bills.

3. Swagbucks

For Swagbucks, you get the chance to earn money doing what you perhaps spend many hours doing browsing the internet. If you create a Swagbucks account, you will receive points for doing simple tasks like shopping online, watching popular videos, and completing surveys within the app. Once you have accumulated enough Swagbucks, you can move on to redeem the points into cash. This is an easy method to convert your everyday browsing habits into a means of earning money to clear your credit card debt fast.

4. Ibotta

While you may focus on paying off debts on your credit cards, you will still need to eat and purchase things. Ibotta can assist you in changing your shopping trips into easy money and paying off your debts. The app will provide you with thousands of rebates for items commonly bought; you only buy an item, scan the receipt and the barcode of the item into your smartphone, and let Ibotta credit your account with the rebate. Once you make $20 or more, you can transfer the money into your PayPal or bank account. This app has different features that will allow you to make extra cash every month, and you will always offer cash rebates to scan a grocery receipt into the app.

5. HQ Trivia

Making some extra cash online is a bit easy, especially when you get an account with HQ Trivia. This is a big online game. When you create an account and play, you will make money for answering the trivia questions of the game correctly. While you accumulate cash in the game, you can easily transfer that to your PayPal account.

6. Acorns

Acorn is a micro-investing firm that builds an investment account for you. This account will link you to one or even more credit cards. Once you buy using the credit card, Acorn will round it up to the nearest dollar and transfer the amount to your investment account. The money that Acorn invests differs depending on the investment risk you want to take. With time, you can accrue a specific value in your Acorns account and ensure you pay off all your debts.

7. Craigslist

This site features "jobs and gigs" where you can find multiple methods to make additional money to pay off debt. You will do everything from odd jobs around the house to tasks that need specific skills like nursing, software engineering, and real estate.

Still, you can use it with other methods to get tutoring work, and so forth.

How much should you pay off towards your debts?

Everyone hates to be in debt, but the fact is that nearly everyone has some debt. Your target should be to have the least amount of debt as possible so that you can save and remain with a lot of cash. The challenge is how to arrive there. You must have realistic expectations and discipline. You can experience peace of mind in that you are in great shape.

Suggestions are quite different on the amount of debt a person has to have and finding your perfect state may take time if you have a big debt. Recommendations on the amount of income that should be directed towards bills and debt will provide you with the groundwork to take control of your debts.

The net income budget

To have a clear picture of the amount of money you need to spend, you should apply your after-tax or net income to decide the percentage that should be directed towards your debts. According to Liz Weston, a personal finance guru for MSN money, individuals reserve 50% of their net income for needs in life, including mortgages, rent, utilities, transportation, and minimum payments on credit cards and loans. Then, 30% of the income is directed to entertainment and other requirements of Weston's budget plan. The other 20% is directed to savings, extra payments, retirement funds, and payments to reduce the percentage of debts.

The debt-to-income ratio

If you go to the bank and request a loan, one of the first things they will want to look before they can grant you the loan is your "debt-to-income ratio". Banks require that your monthly debt payments should not be more than 36% of your gross monthly income. Typically, it has to be about 10%, but if it's lower than 20%, you are still in a good state. In other words, the money you are going to pay out each month for the mortgage, including payments of a credit card, taxes and insurance should not exceed 36%. Before you can start to feel scared, keep in mind that the computation is on your gross income and not the money you take home. The remaining amount has to account for utilities, living expenses, entertainment, clothes, and food.

Mortgage debt

Your monthly mortgage, including your taxes and insurance, has to be over 28% of your monthly gross income. This means, if you earn $4,000 per month, your monthly mortgage debt shouldn't be more than $1,440.

Credit card debt

Unless you make a plan to pay off your credit card debts at the end of every month, they can be a huge problem in your finances. But you will have to stand up and take it. Clear the debts as soon as you can. Once you pay, make sure that you only charge what you can manage to pay full when the statement arrives. This is the reason: the interest that is charged on credit cards is high, and all the money you are paying on interest can be used elsewhere for something important.

Other suggestions

According to the SmartMoney site, the U.S Federal Reserve Board considers a person to be in a financial crisis if the debt obligations are more than 40% of the gross income; however, the website also warns those with a debt of more than 30%. The website says that you may only have 20% of your income to account for taxes when 25% is consumed in debts.

Since the advice on debt management is different from person to person, it is usually hard to know how much of your salary should go toward clearing your debt/s. However, the ultimate thing is to assist you in continuing to reduce your debt and increase your savings. As a result, the best technique recommended is to choose a plan that you are likely to stick with and measure your success using that plan after several months. Adjust the plan as much as you need to in order to cut down your debt/s and increase your savings.

Creating a debt pay off plan that you can stick with

If you want to clear all your debts, you must know how to create a great debt pay off plan, which you can stick with. Here is a step-by-step guide to help you clear your debts:

Know your why

By far, this is the most crucial step, and it doesn't only apply in paying debts but also many other things you want to accomplish in life. In the book *The 7 Habits of Highly Effective People* by Steven Covey, this step is discussed.

The goals you set in life allow you to prioritize many things. Giving yourself time to come up with reasons to explain why you are doing something makes it easier to stick with. Most importantly, something that needs much self-control, such as paying off debt. Maintaining your why in mind will grant you the ability to overcome the different challenges. Additionally, it will assist you in building a debt pay off plan that comprises of your entire goals.

Learning your why and developing an image of what you want to attain and be in life is the main aspect of nurturing good new habits and upholding them.

Depending on your why you may decide to pay all your debts at once, and once you have paid all your debts, make a decision not to accumulate any other debt. Keep in mind that it is impossible to get out of debt if you continue to overspend.

Understand all your debts

Before you can start to create your debt paying approach, you need to understand what you are working with. Start by building a list of all the debts that you owe. This should include all your credit cards, student loans, etc.

Next to every item, write the interest rate, current balance, minimum payment due, and the expected payment date—this date is important to remind you how much longer you have before it expires.

Now that you have an overview of what your debts are, you can come up with a strong decision about your plans with the debt. Depending on your set goals, you may decide to pay some of your debts slowly so that you have enough flexibility.

Build a realistic budget

So far, you know much about your debts; it is time to take a look at your current expenditure in life. This means you must have a budget. Luckily, you have one.

Your budget should include your current living expenditure, such as groceries, car maintenance, and clothing—also include dog food, gifts, and so forth.

When the budget is realistic, you are likely to stick with it, and this will benefit your debt repayment plan. Consider it this way: if you know the amount of money you spend and you choose not to spend in certain areas for the next six months, you will save yourself a lot of money.

When you trim your budget, you save money, which you can then use to pay your debt. In other words, having a realistic budget and sticking with it will highly benefit you in the long run.

Determine the amount you are left with to pay off your debt

At this stage, you already know how your debt appears, and you know the extra cash you have to channel it towards payment of the debt.

Make a quick decision of how fast you want to clear your debt

At this point, you have everything to help you decide what you need to do to pay off your debt. You can decide not to change anything about your current lifestyle and simply clear your debt based on the extra money your budget allows you to have. On the flipside, you may decide to trim your budget and apply for a side job so that you can make extra income to pay off the debt.

The real answer to how fast you want to clear all your debts depends on how fast you want to realize your financial and life goals.

Decide which debts you want to finish first

There are two popular methods used in debt repayment:

"Snowball", where you pay debts beginning with the smallest. The concept behind this method is that small wins will rejuvenate you to continue paying your debts; and

"Debt avalanche", where you have to pay off your debt beginning with the highest interest debts then moving down to the lowest. The advantage of this method is that you will end up paying less interest as time goes on.

Automate your finances

Since you have your debt payment strategy in place, you will want to make it as easy for yourself as possible. One way of doing this is by automating your finances.

Your expenditure should comprise of enough money to deal with your monthly bills; this should comprise of the extra amount you direct towards debts. The account you use to buy things should be linked to the debit card that you apply to your discretionary purchases, such as gas and food.

If you can, let your employer divide your paycheck before it is deposited into your account. If an employer fails to provide you with the option, implement an automatic transfer through your bank.

By applying a hands-off technique to your debt pay off plan, it begins to decrease every month. Your goals will be realized while you concentrate on your day-to-day activities. You will still need to look at your bills and budget to ensure that you remain on track.

Four ways to protect yourself from the unexpected

Don't give room to unexpected expenses to damage your financial plans.

When it comes to unexpected expenses, such as medical bills and car repairs, many of us are always unprepared. And when a financial crisis such as a job loss becomes severe, the less prepared many of us are. According to a study conducted by Pew Charitable Trusts in 2015, half of Americans aren't ready for a financial crisis or unexpected event. Another study by Pew found out that 55% of American homes don't have cash savings to cater for an income of one month. While being scared of the unexpected will keep you awake at night, here are some steps to implement to secure your finances:

1. Understand the condition of your current finances

It is impossible to plan your finances when you don't have a clear understanding of your income and spending. First, you need to define your average monthly income, including any additional money you make. Then outline your average monthly spending; this should comprise of everything—your student loan, car repayment, entertainment, and hobbies. If your income is higher than your expenses, the difference is what you can save for the unexpected. In case your expenses are higher than your income, then you will have to examine your finances and identify methods to cut down on your spending.

2. Set up an emergency debt

Once you develop a clear picture of your finances, then you can compute the least that you require each month to handle your expenses. You can begin by prioritizing your bills. Examine your costs and outline your monthly bills. These are bills that you have to pay every month, such as the mortgage, groceries, utilities, and many more. Next, you should outline your optional expenditures; for example, a gym membership, eating, TV, and Netflix. The total amount of your necessities is what you require each month.

Assess your optional expenditure and find out whether there is something you can reduce. Instead of going out every day to eat, you can change and apply a different option. If you can understand these and many other debt myths, you will gain the confidence to make better financial decisions today that may impact you in the future.

Chapter 3: Saving Money

All of us have strong reasons when it comes to saving money. We like to say that we will begin to save once we attain a specific milestone; for example, when we reach a certain age or get a salary increment, or when children move out.

However, the truth is that you can only begin to save when you build healthy money habits and your future needs are more critical than your wants.

Don't be scared; it is not as hard as it looks. With some changes to your methods of spending, you'll be on the right track to save money.

Why don't many Americans save money?

Everyone knows that they need to save some money for every income they earn, but many people don't save with the knowledge that they are supposed to save. According to a report published by the Federal Reserve, approximately 40% of Americans have the challenge to cover a $400 emergency. The reason is that they have competing goals.

In most cases, the purpose of saving money isn't a big enough priority to slow down buying a new smartphone, TV, or kitchen table. In other words, most people spend their money or get into debt to purchase the latest want. This debt then becomes a monthly payment that may affect paychecks and lives.

Well, what is the goal of saving money?

You can eliminate the habit of living on a paycheck by applying a simple secret: create a zero-based budget before the month starts. A budget requires a person to become intentional. It assists a person in building a plan and identifying where the money is flowing and how much you can save every month. It is never too late to take control of your money.

Reasons why you should consider saving money

Now that credit is very easy to get, you may ask why a person may prefer to save money and make a purchase with real cash. If you want a certain product, you remove your credit card and pay it using a debit card. However, if you know that you can manage to pay the credit at the end of the month, what's the problem? It is unfortunate that many people are buying into this idea. Below are some of the reasons why you need to save:

1. To become independent financially

The metrics for becoming wealthy are based on whom you talk to. Being economically independent may refer to the ability to go on a vacation any time you want, abandoning work and returning to school to change careers, or even investing in another person's start-up. This may also mean taking a lesser job that you feel satisfied with financially, or retiring when you want to instead of working because you have no choice otherwise.

Financial independence is different from being rich. Having savings that you can depend on is what shows how "rich" you are regardless of how you define it.

2. Save 50% on anything you purchase

If you use your credit to purchase products and delay to pay for the credit at the end of the month, then you are perhaps paying higher interest for the lateness. It is important to stop relying on credit cards if you want to save up. Savings will allow you to buy items when they are put on sale and spend time on making better decisions. When you buy products using real money, you tend to save about 50% of what you could have paid as interest to credit card companies.

3. Purchase a car

Before you can buy a new car, you have to make a down payment first to help you get an affordable interest rate. While you can get this money from your credit card, the interest charged is a bit high. However, when you save some money, you can use it to make a down payment that will allow you to reduce the interest that you will have to pay.

4. Purchase a home

It is hard for a bank to offer you some cash to buy a house if you don't pay some down payment, and you aren't allowed to borrow a down payment. You need to have this money kept, saved, or have a person assist you with but not lend you. A down payment should be about 5% of the buying price of the house, and then the bank will decide whether to lend you the remaining 95%. There are different costs and fees that you are required to pay when you purchase a home; that means you need an extra 5% for those expenditures.

5. Emergencies

Though we remain optimistic that emergencies will not arise, the truth is that they do happen. A family member might develop a health problem that may require an emergency trip to the hospital, or an accident may occur, or bad weather may flood and crack pipes, or you may have to take a flight to attend the funeral of a loved one. These kinds of emergencies are quite expensive; that is the reason why it's important to be prepared.

6. You can lose your job

When having good moments, everyone believes that their job is protected, but on bad days, many start to understand that evil things can occur to anyone. You can wake up and lose your job or even experience an accident. Employment Insurance (EI) starts to hit you after six weeks. That is the reason why you need to have some savings. If you don't have any savings, you will have to use a credit card which is going to be more expensive.

7. To have a better life

There are a lot of emotional, physical, and psychological effects that occur when you live a stressful life.

There is some truth to the saying that happiness also comes from being organized. There's much in your future that doesn't apply to your spending, but simply become organized and be in charge of your future.

8. Unforeseen expenses

What will you do in case your car requires significant repairs? Are you capable of raising $500-$3,000 instantly? Suppose your house needs a major renovation? You can look forward to the bank giving you some cash for all these things.

Don't wait for anything; start today by putting aside a little money every time you get paid until you have an emergency saving fund of between $500-$1000.

How to make money while sleeping?

You can save tons of money in your daily life from negotiating bills to limiting your spending. Even while you are asleep, saving money shouldn't stop.

Turn plugs off

Besides the fridge, freezer, and alarm clock, there's nothing you need to leave plugged in overnight. Before you head to the land of slumber, take a quick look around and ensure everything is switched off or unplugged.

Make this your nighttime routine. Walk from room to room to ensure that the kettle, microwave, toaster, DVD player, and TV are off.

It may not look like a big saving, but over the year, it will add up.

No opportunity to shop

Everyone has done this. Late in the evening, when there seems to be nothing on the television, you start to browse on the internet and view your favorite online shops. It is during this time that you order those pair of jeans, book a holiday and many other things.

If there is nothing on television, or you have nothing to do, go to bed early. If you are sound asleep, you will have no means to spend money, and you will protect your money from unnecessary spending.

Look at the taps

Have you ever been resting in bed when you heard the sound of a dripping tap in your house? Instead of continuing to enjoy your sleep, get up and sort it out. Not only is the sound of a dripping tap very annoying but it is also like throwing money down the drain.

Once you switch off the tap, you can sleep quietly without any distractions while knowing that your water bills won't be affected.

You will eat little

When you have a great night's sleep, not only will you feel refreshed in the morning, but it will help you to eat effectively. In other words, a better night's sleep will allow you to save money on the cost of food.

A research done by the University of Chicago discovered that subjects who decided to sleep for only four hours for two nights had an 18% drop in leptin, a hormone that sends the signal to the brain that there is no more food, and a 28% increase in ghrelin, a hormone that activates hunger.

In other words, enough sleep results in eating less food.

The myth of financial advisors

When you consider the idea of a "financial advisor", do you imagine a rich person resting in a posh office? Many people do, and rich people tend to employ financial advisors to help them manage their finances. However, financial advisors aren't meant for the rich alone.

If you aren't wealthy, you may think that you are doing everything fine to manage your finances, including saving each month and setting aside money for your retirement plan. This is a great start; however, that isn't enough. Having a professional may become critical if you don't have much cash to work with.

Experienced portfolio managers and retired officers can assist you to save and invest money. Maybe it is time to think about listening to what experts say.

There are just moments in life when you need an expert. Maybe you inherited a large sum of cash, or you received a settlement of a certain size. You may even have won the lottery. You understand managing a huge sum of cash isn't meant for amateurs. What about if all that comes to your bank account is your paycheck? Do you need a financial expert? Perhaps you should ask yourself the following questions:

- Do you have children about to go to college?

- Are you planning to get married soon, or are you recently divorced?

- Would you prefer to begin a business?

- Do you plan to retire at a certain point?

- Do you feel anxious about your financial future?

If you said "yes" to any of the above questions, consider looking for help.

The ten myths about financial advisors

Wall Street has a sophisticated marketing style that will persuade you to purchase their products, financial advice, and services. One technique is to take control of your assets.

There are facts and myths. As you are going to see, the myths generate substantial risk when you choose financial advisors and implement their advice. The more you are aware of myths, the more prepared you will be to secure your financial interests:

1. Financial advisors, sales representatives, and planners are all the same

This is simply not true. There is a big difference in quality-based services, education, certifications, compliance records, conflicts of interest, and other essential considerations. This difference builds a significant financial risk when you choose an advisor.

2. Experts must have the least amount of experience before they can deliver financial advice

The reality is that there are no minimum experience requirements for advisors. They can start selling financial services and products on the same day they get their licenses.

3. Advisors should have a college degree

There is no minimum education qualification for advisors.

4. Advisors should have a clean record of compliance to sell financial services, products, and advice.

A financial advisor can have numerous complaints on their records and still get the current licenses.

5. There are minimum requirements to refer yourself as a financial planner

This is also not true; anyone can become a financial planner regardless of whether they have the required experience or not.

6. Advisors working for main companies have safer choices than those who work for smaller companies

Big companies pay billions of dollars as a penalty for deceiving investors. Big companies have multiple, hidden conflicts of interest.

7. Advisors who receive compensation with commissions offer "free" advice and services

There is nothing like free advice and free services. Advisors receive commissions to sell investment and insurance products. The companies that generate products set the fees that they charge, or add deferred sales charges to compensate for the commissions they receive.

8. Older financial experts have more experience than young advisors

Wall Street companies assume that old advisors have more experience. As a result, they look for older advisors to build the notion of experience. This is the wrong sales practice.

Wealth management isn't just for the rich

Investing and management of wealth isn't meant for people such as Robert Kuok, who is considered among the richest people in Malaysia with assets worth USD 12 billion. It is important for middle-aged individuals to plan for retirement, and young couples to prepare for the education of their children.

Typically, wealthy management involves a mix of investment and financial planning. Investment refers to the practice of converting proportional investments into bonds, which involve security selection, asset mix selection, and monitoring.

On the other hand, financial planning describes the science of arranging economic issues, such as expenses, wills, estate planning, insurance, and lending. Both have a similar goal of realizing personal objectives.

With the purpose to accrue and preserve, wealth experts implement a financial plan based on the needs of the individual. As a result, it is reasonable to include all aspects of financial needs and status to build an efficient money management structure.

When done correctly, one can reduce the risks in investment, unnecessary expenses, taxes, and improving financial returns and boosting assets. It is necessary for enabling efficient use of assets during the lifetime of a person and transfer of assets at the time of death.

Why isn't the management of wealth just for the rich?

Managing your cash allows you to understand the way you can invest and save to fulfill different financial goals. This will help you to preserve wealth and control your expenses.

Sustainable retirement

Everyone should have a plan for retirement whether they are working in the public sector or self-employed. Based on a survey conducted by the Ministry of Human resources, about 14% of retirees finish their savings within the first three years of retirement, 5% within five years, and 70% within ten years.

To enjoy your retirement, you need to have sufficient savings to take care of your expenses and generate streams of passive income.

An expert in wealth management will advise you on the best methods for saving up for your future. If you aren't enrolled in the pension, you can begin to save for your retirement by using a private retirement scheme.

Save for your children's education

There is no bigger gift than educating your kids. The cost of education can be a bit high at private colleges, and so you need to have some savings.

For you to save and make sufficient money to cater for the education needs of your children, you are required to consider various investments that will suit their needs and risk tolerance. A wealth manager will recommend the best plan of action. Some of the available opportunities include capital financing, unit trusts, and bonds.

Those who don't mind the risk can invest in gold, commodities, and FOREX. These investments feature a big risk, but they can deliver significant long-term returns to investors.

Ensure that your family is secure financially

Insurance plays a big role in financial planning. It is essential to have enough insurance coverage to make sure that your family is financially secure against emergencies. Depending on the needs, it is possible to invest in medical insurance, life insurance, and many other options.

The goal isn't just to find insurance coverage but to look for sufficient coverage. With the right management in place, an individual may be aware of the total insured that is sufficient depending on the affordability and commitments.

Making sure that your wealth is passed on smoothly

Wealth management, when handled in the right way, can increase your money and assets. As a result, it is important to make sure that assets are assigned to the right persons if anything bad was to go wrong.

Highlight your investment beneficiaries to make sure that hard-earned investments go to your loved ones with the least legal formalities. It will be a time of grief, and it won't be okay to put them through the challenge of organizing the finances.

Control your short-term goals

You probably have short-term goals, such as purchasing a car, saving for a down payment on a house, or even furnishing the new home. To achieve these goals, you want to think about share financing and fixed deposits, as they deliver high liquidity and have a lower risk based on the short timeline.

A balanced wealth management system should include long-term and short-term goals before generating an effective plan to fulfill all the objectives based on the current potential.

It's for everyone

This means that money management plays a key role in achieving personal and financial dreams by implementing a diverse approach, which allows us to make plans for a better set of opportunities and risks.

Automatic Investing

Automatic investing is when you agree for a fixed amount of money to be cut from your paycheck every month and spent in a pre-determined allocation. The contribution that goes to the retirement plan is a great example. If your employer withdraws some cash from your paycheck every month and invests in the 401K, then you have automated your investment.

How can you automate investing?

This is a simple process. The first thing is to decide the amount of money you want to save and from which account. The next thing is to get in touch with your investment provider and let them be aware that you want to create an automatic investment strategy and how you want to invest the money.

Why Automatic Investing is a great idea

1. It's hard to spend the money

When you draft money automatically into your investment account, that means you can't get tempted to spend it. This will reduce discretionary spending and allow you to fulfill your financial goals.

2. Fewer arguments

Once your investment is automated, it is then possible to automate your savings, and that offers minimum room to fight for the amount to spend and is money kept for your future without any work. In other words, you don't need to convince your other partner of retirement planning.

3. No work is needed

It requires the least amount of effort to set up. Once everything is okay, your financial success will deal with everything. You will not waste time calling, being worried, and moving around. The money will be invested as you focus on other important things.

4. The odds are in your favor

Many people have their savings and investments in their retirement plans. There are two main explanations for this: first, tax penalties make it hard and expensive to use the money; secondly, the money will increase fast every month because you will be adding each month.

Though you can use your non-retirement account without suffering tax penalties, many people don't touch the automated accounts; they leave them to grow. Automating your investment is very simple, and the payoff is immense. It has additional benefits of securing your future, reducing your current spending, and cutting down your financial friction at home.

Building a smart investment portfolio

Many investors want to build investments that will deliver growth and income that is required to fulfill financial goals. To achieve that, you have to understand yourself as an investor. And the reason for this is that a portfolio that is good for someone else may not work for you. Below are some of the factors that you need to consider when building a smart investment portfolio:

- Your goals
- Your age
- The time for your different goals
- Your attitude towards risk

You also need to master ideas related to asset allocation. After this, you can begin to look into your investment selections and how different types of investments utilize your money. Your ability to endure risk, asset allocation, and diversification are the main aspects of your portfolio.

Investments for different times

Some of the reasons for defining investment goals is to help you know when you will require money to pay for them. The investment method you choose should be different based on the time you invest your money. Goals can be short term, long term, and middle term.

Saving for something big using goals

If you have a dream that you know you can accomplish, if only you had the means, then saving is something that you should consider. To help you realize your dream, below are tips to assist you with the saving part of the equation.

If you only consider debts for true value and investments, you could feel like you don't have the money to accomplish the things you love. However, a smart saving plan may assist you to accomplish all of your dreams. Additionally, you will understand more about your finances.

These tips will help you save between $1,000-$5,000:

1. Create a budget

Your dream may cost more or less, and that is why you need to create a budget in advance. This will help you to outline your plans correctly. Go online and look at existing budgets for projects, trips, and hobbies. Do some research to have a rough idea.

2. Determine your savings rate

You need to know how much you can raise in a day, week, or per pay period. This step has two major sections: monitoring your spending and looking at areas where you can reduce. If you have never monitored your spending before, look for a guide. Monitoring your spending is always a great idea because you will get a rough idea of how much you spend. If you don't have the time, you can approximate by looking at your weekly, monthly, or annual bills.

Once you develop a great idea of your cash flow, find ways to spend less. Saving doesn't mean that you deny yourself everything, so you should not start by being ruthless. But take the time to think of ways in which you can cut down your expenditure without denying yourself the joy of living. Even if it's saving $50, that will add up with time.

> i) A great starting point is your routine bills. Ask yourself what amount of money you want to spend on your internet, car insurance, phone plan, and cable. And how much can you save when you negotiate or go for a less expensive product. The work you put into your savings will pay off after a month.
>
> ii) Once you review your routine expenses, shift to your discretionary expenses. Small purchases can be quite expensive. If you know where your money is going, then you can decide whether to reduce the cost or go for a cheaper option. If you find it difficult to get a perfect item, ask

yourself why you need that product. Maybe the item isn't that important to you, and you could even create a homemade option.

iii) If cutting down on your spending doesn't seem to work fast, you can think of increasing your income. In this case, you look for ways to earn extra income. You can consider doing some freelance work every week.

Determine the period when you will be done with saving

Once you know how much you need, and how fast you can make it, then determining when you will be done shouldn't be hard at all.

Save on autopilot

Until this point, you have accomplished the hard part of building a plan and making tough decisions. What you really need is to move on with your normal life of cutting down on your costs and earning more. The money will slowly increase. It is advised that you spend time every week to evaluate your progress. Saving can include sacrifices if you are going to change your habits of living. Take some time to write down the reasons why you are saving and watch yourself getting closer to your goal.

Be flexible

You may manage to stick to the initial plan. Or you could encounter unexpected challenges. Sometimes, it pays to change your behavior. If the groceries cost more than expected, then it is reasonable to spend less on restaurants.

If you are behind on a goal, or you have to get some money to pay for an emergency, don't be scared; it's simple to adjust. If you think you may need more time, you can update your goal accordingly.

Celebrate

When you achieve your goals, take the time to appreciate your achievement. Savings require persistence and sacrifice. That is why you need to be proud of what you have accomplished.

Chapter 4: Managing Your Personal Finances in a Stress-Free Way

The importance of money management

Do you find yourself with different credit cards, a mortgage, and an auto loan?

There are methods to help you make this manageable. It takes time to discover the ins and outs of it and twist your budget so that it can satisfy your needs:

1. You know where your money is going

Once you budget your money and decide to stick to the budget, you will be able to monitor where your money goes at the end of each month. This is a huge benefit since it will allow you to watch the way you spend money and save more. You can track your spending for several months and then balance the budget to assign a lot of money to savings, or even retirement.

If you handle your money well, you will manage to make early payments, and avoid surpassing the limit on the credit card.

When you stick to your budget, these methods will assist you to save money.

This prevents you from spending much money.

2. A better plan of retirement

When you save now and manage your money in the right way, it will benefit you in the long term. First, it will force you to look into the future and look into your retirement plans.

When you implement your money management skills, you will be building yourself a strong retirement plan. The money that you save and invest will grow as time goes by.

3. Allows you to concentrate on your goals

You will avoid unnecessary expenditure that doesn't support achieving financial goals. If you are dealing with limited resources, budgeting makes it complex to fulfill your ends.

4. You organize your spending and savings

When you divide your income into different types of expenditure and savings, a budget will allow you to remain aware of the type of expenditure that drains the portion of your money. This way, it is simple for you to set adjustments. Good money management acts as a reference for organizing receipts, bills, and financial statements. Once you organize all your financial transactions, you will save effort and time.

5. You can speak to your partner about money

If you do share your income with your spouse, then a budget can be the best tool to show how money is spent. This increases teamwork to work on a common financial target and prevents arguments on the way money is used. Creating a budget together with your spouse will help you to avoid conflict and eliminate personal conflicts on the way money is spent.

6. It determines whether you can take on debt and how much

Taking on debt isn't a bad thing, but it is important, especially if you cannot afford it. A budget will indicate the amount of debt load you can take on without getting stressed.

7. Allows you to generate additional money

When you budget, you get the chance to single out and eliminate unnecessary spendings, such as on penalties, late fees, and interests. These little savings can increase with time.

A budget refers to a plan that takes into account your monthly cash flow and outflow. This is a snapshot of what you own, and what you expect to spend, and which will allow you to realize your financial goals by assisting you in highlighting your saving and spending.

Creating a budget is the most crucial aspect of financial planning. The amount of money you have doesn't indicate how much money you make, but instead, it is how effective your budgeting is. If you want to take care of your finances, then you will have to understand where your money is flowing to. Contrary to popular belief that budgeting is hard, it isn't, and it doesn't eliminate the fun from your life. A budget will save you from an unexpected financial crisis and a life of debt.

Many people have hopes of becoming rich, but they don't have a clue about how to accumulate wealth or where to start. You can begin by learning how to create a budget. A budget is important because it will assist you to start accumulating wealth and accomplishing your goals. Below are some steps to budgeting:

1. Monitor your expenses and income

The first thing to building a budget is to determine the amount of money you have and what you are spending it on. By monitoring your expenses, you will manage to classify how you spend your money. Planning how you spend your money is critical because you can tell how much you want to spend in every category. You can monitor your income and expenses by creating a journal, spreadsheet, or cash book. Every time you make money, you can monitor it as income, and every time you spend money, you can track it as an expense.

If you use a debit card, try to track back three months of your spending to get a comprehensive picture of your expenditure.

2. Evaluate your income

The next stage is to assess your income. You can do this by computing the amount of income you get via gifts, scholarships, etc.

3. Determine your expenses

Once you know your monthly income, next is to determine the total of your expenses. First, you need to define what your fixed, variable expenses are. Fixed expenses, sales, and bills have the same price every month. The fixed expenses comprise of car payments, internet, and rent. Variable expenses refer to costs that change, such as utilities and groceries.

Be sure to include payments of debt in your budget. Find out the amount that you can contribute towards your debts to make sure that you are on the correct path to financial stability. Handling debts and savings go hand in hand.

4. Don't forget about savings

It is quite easy to forget to save money. Keep in mind that you always pay yourself first. Give it a try using 10-20% of your income savings. Since savings increase, you can choose to include money that you didn't spend in the budget to save.

Building a saving strategy

Many people know how to manage the little money they get when the month ends, but they find it hard to save when they have a tight budget. If you look at finance articles online, you will see different types of saving methods—right from freezing all spending to packing your own lunch for a month. But how can you determine which ones work? In this section, you will learn easy money-saving strategies you can implement and how you can make them work for you:

1. Eat out less

It is a fact that eating out is expensive. Even a cup of coffee every day adds up. The cup of coffee may cost you $2, but if you calculate it over a year, that is over $700. In other words, if you continue to eat out every day, you will be spending a lot.

How it works

In a Claris survey, it was found out that 43% of respondents accepted a cutback on eating out, and 33% reported to save money. More than three out of four people who attempted this particular method reported positive results. Though this is not as effective as using a budget, it does save something.

How can you implement it?

If you are eating out every day because you don't know how to cook great food, it is high time that you changed that habit. And don't be worried because learning how to cook is pretty easy. Nowadays, you can turn to YouTube and other online food channels to learn how to prepare different kinds of food. Search for your favorite recipes and begin to follow each step of the preparation.

Remember: cooking food at home doesn't really mean that you need to start everything from scratch. You can choose to purchase chicken broth in a jar. Even if you are going to buy most of these ingredients, a meal prepared at home is going to be cheap.

Even when you have the above ingredients ready, a home prepared meal is cheaper than one from a restaurant.

2. Save loose change

Have a loose change jar. Any time you go shopping and are given coins as change, throw the coins into the jar.

3. Stay out of debt

Being debt free will help you to save cash; if you can pay off all your debt, you will get the chance to organize your debt.

How it works

The stats on eliminating debt can be shocking. For example, the Claris poll showed that only 22% of people attempted this strategy, and 26% reported that it worked for them. In other words, this strategy can help you save money.

Staying out of debt can save you a good sum of cash, but many people find it hard to pay off their debts.

4. Be a minimalist

Adopting a minimalist approach is a type of voluntary simplicity. It requires a person to cut down on costs so that they concentrate on what is important. A minimalist's life generally means owning a smaller house, fewer "toys", and fewer clothes. But it also implies minimal work and more time to do the things that you like.

How does it happen?

This is a great saving strategy that works even for those who don't want to use it. A minimalist approach can be the effect of other methods to save. In most cases, many people scaled their life to stick to their budget. Then, with time, they discovered that their simple lifestyle helped them save more.

How do you do it?

There are various misconceptions about minimalism. A blog about minimalism jokes that minimalists live in small apartments and don't have jobs, cars, TVs, or more than 100 objects.

The purpose of minimalism is to free yourself from issues in life that aren't important. It is not focused on sacrifice; it merely involves eliminating things that you don't want to have in life or creating room for things that you care about. As a result, living with fewer items can make you feel satisfied.

The best thing with living a simple lifestyle is that there is no right or wrong way of doing it. This means that you can become a minimalist by staying in an off-the-grid cabin and make your own food. Or you can stay in an urban loft and walk every day while heading to work. The philosophy of minimalism requires that you concentrate less on the things you have and more on what you do with your life.

If you aren't sure whether you can deal with this kind of life, you can start small and slowly identify a few things in your life that you don't want. For example, if your wardrobe is filled with many things, perhaps throw out or donate some clothes. Or if you spend a lot of time online, plan to reduce your screen time.

Whatever you decide to do, make sure that you don't simplify your life by surrendering on the things you value or treasure; instead, choose things that require the most work for the least reward.

If you are searching for methods to help you save a lot of money, these methods are the best ones to begin with. Since they have worked for other people, there is a big chance that they will work for you too. However, make sure that you don't jump in and try all the methods at once—just select strategies that you believe may work for you.

For example, if you enjoy eating out, as it makes you happy, eliminating this option may not work for you. You will perhaps get disappointed and give up in a few weeks. So, instead of cutting down on eating out, you can decide to look for something different to scale down on.

In general, the purpose is to avoid debt. If your main goal in life is to own a home, don't give up on that and try to avoid a mortgage debt. You can hunt for a house that you will easily manage to pay for, even if it means spending two more years paying for it.

If you aren't sure of the savings style to try, creating a budget is perhaps the best approach. The best thing about budgets is that you don't adjust them to suit your goals; however, you can decide to spend less on your car so that you can get a better house.

Investing your money

Investing your money gives you a chance to grow your money, and even make more than what you have. However, not everyone who decides to invest their money makes profits; some have lost tons of money in the process. There is a different way to invest your money, and this section will introduce you to some of the most common strategies for investment:

Stock investment

If you want to become a stock investor, you need to have a proven strategy for investing in the stock market. You will realize that long-term success begins with learning how to maintain the odds in your favor and control the possible risks.

Understand that for starting investors and seasoned stock market investors, it is impossible to purchase and sell the best stocks at the right time. However, also learn that you don't need to be right to generate money. You simply need to understand the basic rules for how to select the best stocks to watch and the right time to purchase the best stocks at the right time.

Experts in the stock market will tell you that it's hard to time the market, although it's unrealistic to assume that you'll get at the very bottom and out at the very top of a market cycle. There are different methods to identify major changes that occur in the market trends as they arise. When you recognize some of these changes, you can get ready to make substantial profits in a new market.

New investors in the stock market tend to focus on the type of stocks to purchase and ignore the most pertinent issues of when to sell. This is a huge mistake. Without a set of great rules, you might give back all your hard-earned gains.

Typically, there are two major rules that you need to adhere to: the offensive rules of locking your profits, and the defensive rules of cutting down on losses.

Investing online

Online investing can be a quick and convenient method that is more affordable than other methods. But before you can handle your online investment, you need to ask yourself several questions:

What type of investor are you?

Online investing is designed for everyone. By choosing this option, you hold the responsibility to research all investments and make all investment decisions regarding your online account. If you don't feel okay as that kind of investor, you could be comfortable working with a financial advisor. If you like to manage your investment portfolio and feel secure that you have enough knowledge, you may decide to go with online investment.

What type of account do you want to open?

There are various types of online accounts to select from, including joint and individual accounts. The type of account you select will rely on the kind of objectives you have set and how you want to invest.

What company and type of security are you interested in?

For the self-directed investors, it is important to do your homework well because you get some payment for it. There is some level of risk related to all types of investments, so you may want to perform some research to make the right investment decision.

Some tips before investing:

> 1. Anyone can invest in the stock market, but it's important to save money for retirement and emergencies first.

2. Many people will see significant profits from investing abroad rather than attempting to play the stock market from day to day.

3. If you don't want to trade individual's stocks, begin small, and do your research. Don't just follow advice from famous investors.

Real estate investment

If you want to learn another method to build wealth, then you will have to consider real estate investment. This may seem like an excellent idea, especially if you come from a place where the real estate market is booming. However, you need to be prepared for the commitment.

Real estate demands that you commit your time, and that is why you need to understand it before you start. It is bad to invest in something which you don't have much knowledge about.

Whether real estate investment is a great idea or not, it all depends on you, and your financial abilities. Additionally, your goals will also determine whether you need to invest in real estate. Not every investment is for everyone, but it can be a big tool for growing wealth when done in the right manner.

Types of real estate investment

If you thought that real estate investment is tied only to renting and owning property, then you need to think again. There are basically different methods of investing in real estate, and some of those methods don't require renters.

Ownership of a home

You can purchase a house to invest in. However, there's a slight difference between owning a house and investing in real estate properties. When you invest in a house, you will not make money actively or even increase your monthly cash flow of the property.

The truth is that paying for your house is one of the most important long-term investments you can make.

Invest in Fundrise

Many people want to get into real estate investing, but don't want to handle tenants, repairs, or even manage payments. Fortunately, you can place your money in real estate investment without worrying about doing all the management.

Fundrise is an online investment platform which will give you the chance to invest your cash in real estate investment. It is controlled by Fundrise professionals, while your role is to watch as your money grows.

Why go for Fundrise? It's easy, and they have a track record of excellent returns. Since they can guarantee profits, they are a reputable firm to invest with.

Another reason why most people like to invest with Fundrise is that it's easy to start using it. Also, they will assist you in determining the type of investments that are best for you.

Depending on your response, they will either suggest:

- Long-term growth
- Supplemental income
- Balanced investing

With a minimum of $500, you can invest in Fundrise, or with a minimum of $1,000, you can start to invest in Fundrise income eReit. They have the lowest fees for investment via their site, but the returns are quite reasonable.

Buy rental houses to make income

This is another method you can use to build wealth in the long term. The same reasons why you need to own a home should move you to purchase a property. However, investment in real estate gives you the added advantage of income.

At the least, the rent that you get on investment property has to cover the costs of owning it. When the rent is more than your costs, the property will produce a positive cash flow.

If it does generate a positive cash flow, then the income can come to you as tax-free. The reason is that you can take depreciation expenses on the house. Because it is an investment property, you have permission to "expense" the improvements after some time.

Some things that you should know about rental properties include:

- They require a large down payment, about 20% more of the buying price.
- There are vacancy aspects.
- Repairs and maintenance.
- Earning a mortgage on an investment property rather than the owner-occupied property is hard.

Each of the above factors can be solved, but you must know that owning a property isn't that easy. If you want a lower risk history, rental properties may not be the best investment option for you.

Invest in commercial real estate

This is another variation of rental property which entails investing in retail and office property. It assumes a similar pattern—you buy a property and then rent it out to tenants, who will pay your mortgage and hopefully make some returns.

Commercial real estate investing is generally complicated and expensive compared to investing in rental property in the residential section

But why should you invest in real estate at a commercial level?

The concept of risk versus reward shows that commercial real estate is a lucrative investment because of the huge profits that can be made from it.

On the other hand, commercial real estate usually requires long-term leases. Because the property is going to be rented out as a business, they may require a multi-year lease. This will support the continuity of the business.

Appreciation on a property can also be higher than for residential property. This is prominent when the property generates a large return. And it is likely to be the case for commercial property because the tenant will pay for the maintenance of the building.

Leases can be designed to offer the landlord a given percentage of profits for the business.

The drawback of commercial properties is that they are often subjected to the business cycle. In times of recessions, the business revenue may decrease, and the tenant may have a massive problem in paying for the rent.

Investing in commercial real estate should be for experienced investors who have a huge risk of tolerance.

How to detail your financial goals?

Below are the steps to follow to set up your financial goals:

>1. Identify what is important to you. Put everything on the table and inspect it.
>
>2. Filter everything that is within reach, what will require more time, and what should be part of a long-term plan.
>
>3. Use the SMART goal method.
>
>4. Develop a realistic budget. Get a clear picture of the flow of your money and then work to focus on that specific goal.
>
>5. Track your progress.

Examples of financial goals:

1. Create a budget and stick with it.

Some people are shy of the budgeting process. Though you get rich by concentrating on assets and income, experts say that a budget is useful if you want to control how much you spend.

2. Pay off your credit card debt

When setting your financial goals, this should be among your goals. The interest charges on your credit card consume much of your cash flow that could be used somewhere else. Once you clear all your credit card debt, you should be conscious enough not to use the credit card that much.

3. Set up an emergency account

4. Save for your retirement plan

Delayed gratification is a rare feature of many Americans. However, we need to have a retirement plan where we save for the future.

5. Live according to your means

If you do spend more than what you earn, then you will have a lot of debt to pay. If you spend less than your income, you have savings.

6. Nurture skills to increase your income

It doesn't really mean going back to college. It could just mean getting some extra training at your current job. It could also imply looking for a mentor who can deliver tips and feedback. It may also imply going to attend workshops and conferences, or even networking in your job.

7. Have a down payment for your house

For most people, investing in a house is a huge investment. The more the down payment is, the more flexibility and freedom will be given for the entire period of the loan.

8. Increase your credit score

For you to get that house or any other purchase that needs a loan, you have to qualify for a much lower interest rate. In other words, a high credit score saves you a lot of money to be eligible for lower interest rates.

The main point is that everyone can do more than what they think they can, and we need to plan for our financial future.

Accomplishing your financial goals

The right way to achieve your goals is to generate a plan that will prioritize your goals.

When you review your goals, you will realize that some are narrow while others are broad. You can classify your goals into:

> 1. Short-term financial goals, which require less than a year to accomplish. An example is purchasing a new refrigerator.
>
> 2. Mid-term goals can be realized instantly but should not take many years to achieve. Examples include completing a degree and buying a car.
>
> 3. Long-term goals may take many years to achieve. Examples include buying a house and saving for a child's college education.

The process of setting goals requires making a decision of the type of goals you want to achieve and approximating the size of money needed and other needed resources.

Create a goal chart

Creating a financial goal chart is the best way to begin your process of investment. Below are five steps that can be useful to help you build your goal chart:

> 1. Note down your financial goal. It has to be measurable, specific, realistic, and contain a timeline.

2. Determine whether you have set a short-term, mid-term, or long-term goal. This can change depending on your condition.

3. Determine the amount of money that you need to achieve your goal.

4. Brainstorm methods that you can use to attain your goal while cutting down on your expenses.

5. Choose the best ways to fulfill your goals and note them down.

Conclusion

Your credit score will affect your potential purchasing of significant items, such as a car or house. As a result, it is important to have a healthy credit score that will deliver to you the freedom to enjoy life. If you have a bad credit score, and you want to build it back to a good score, first, you have to know what you are working with. Look for a copy of your credit report via different free sources. Once you have the copy, look for errors and open account balances.

When you have a good credit score, you tend to have peace of mind and can start saving for the future. Saving for your future is critical, and that is why you need to begin "thinking lean", which will show you opportunities to become creative and reduce your expenditure.

Keep in mind that by saving today, you will be preparing for a great future when you grow old. Now that you have come to the end of the book don't stop now—start putting into practice everything that you have learned. Creating a budget, setting your financial goals, and eliminating things that eat out your expenditure is the sure way to realize the objectives of this book.

www.ingramcontent.com/pod-product-compliance
Lightning Source LLC
LaVergne TN
LVHW040051080526
838202LV00045B/3576